Questions
young people ask
answers that work

VOLUME 1

this book is the property of

_____

Publishers
WATCHTOWER BIBLE AND TRACT SOCIETY OF NEW YORK, INC.
Brooklyn, New York, U.S.A.
2011 Printing

This publication is not for sale. It is provided as part of a worldwide
Bible educational work supported by voluntary donations

Unless otherwise indicated, Scripture quotations are from the modern-language
New World Translation of the Holy Scriptures—With References

The names of some of the youths in this book have been changed

Photo Credits: Page 241: © Gusto Productions/Photo Researchers, Inc.; page 244: mouth cancer:
© Mediscan/Visuals Unlimited, Inc.; clogged artery: © Index Stock/Photolibrary; cancerous lung:
© Arthur Glauberman/Photo Researchers, Inc.; page 245: MRI of brain: © Mediscan/Visuals Unlimited,
Inc.; cancerous kidney: © Dr. E. Walker/Photo Researchers, Inc.

Questions Young People Ask—Answers That Work, Volume 1   English (_yp1_-E)
Made in the United States of America

Answers That Work!

'How can I communicate with my parents?' 'How can I make friends?' 'What's wrong with casual sex?' 'Why do I get so sad?'

If you've asked yourself such questions, you're not alone. Depending on where you've turned for guidance, you may have been given conflicting answers. To help young people get solid advice they can rely on, *Awake!* magazine launched the Bible-based series entitled "Young People Ask . . . " in January 1982. Decades later, the series still draws an enthusiastic response. Each article is the product of extensive research. In fact, to determine just how young people think and feel, *Awake!* writers have spoken to hundreds of youths all over the world! More important, though, the advice given in "Young People Ask" is based on God's Word, the Bible.

The book you now hold was originally published in 1989. However, the chapters have been completely revised to address the issues of today. More than 30 chapters have been adapted from "Young People Ask" articles that were published between 2004 and 2011.

Questions Young People Ask—Answers That Work, Volume 1, will provide you with the tools you need to become a responsible adult. It is our hope that as you apply its advice, you will join the millions of people, both young and adult, who "through use have their perceptive powers trained to distinguish both right and wrong." —Hebrews 5:14.

The Publishers

this book contains . . .

 key scriptures that highlight main points

 TIP

practical suggestions that will help you succeed

DID YOU KNOW . . .

facts that will stimulate your thinking

action plan!

✎ opportunities to express how you will put the material to use

WHAT DO YOU THINK?

● questions that will help you reason on what you've read

in addition . . .

my journal

each section of this book ends with a journal page that will allow you to put your thoughts into words

ROLE MODEL

selected Bible characters are featured as worthy of imitation

contents

1 DEALING WITH FAMILY

How can I talk to my parents?

"I tried really hard to tell my parents how I felt, but it didn't come out right—and they just cut me off. It took a lot for me to get up the nerve to express myself, and it was a complete failure!"—Rosa.

WHEN you were younger, your parents were probably the first ones you ran to for advice. You told them any news, big or small. You freely expressed your thoughts and feelings, and you had confidence in their advice.

Now, though, you might feel that your parents just can't relate to you anymore. "One evening at mealtime I began to cry and pour out my feelings," says a girl named Edie. "My parents *listened*, but they didn't seem to *understand*."

The result? "I just went to my bedroom and cried some more!"

On the other hand, sometimes you might prefer *not* to open up to your parents. "I talk to my parents about many subjects," says a boy named Christopher. "But I like it that sometimes they don't know *everything* I'm thinking."

Is it wrong to keep some thoughts to yourself? Not necessarily—as long as you're not being deceitful. (Proverbs 3: 32) Nevertheless, whether your parents don't seem to understand you or you are holding back, one thing is certain: You need to talk to your parents—and they need to hear from you.

Keep Talking!

In some ways, communicating with your parents is like driving a car. If you encounter a roadblock, you don't give up; you simply find another route. Consider two examples.

ROADBLOCK 1 You need to talk, but your parents don't seem to be listening. "I find it difficult to communicate with my father," says a girl named Leah. "Sometimes I'll talk to him for a while and then he'll say, 'I'm sorry, were you speaking to me?'"

QUESTION: What if Leah really needs to discuss a problem? She has at least three options.

Just as a roadblock need not be a dead end, you can find a way to get through and communicate with your parents!

Yell at her dad. Leah screams: "Come on, this is important! Listen!"

Option **A**

Stop talking to her dad. Leah simply gives up trying to talk about her problem.

Option **B**

Wait for a better time and bring up the subject again. Leah speaks with her dad face-to-face later, or she writes him a letter about her problem.

Option **C**

Which option do *you* think Leah should choose? ✎ ....

Let's explore each option to see where it would likely lead.

Leah's dad is distracted—and thus unaware of her frustration. So if Leah chooses **Option A,** her screaming might seem to come out of nowhere. This option probably won't make Leah's dad more receptive to her words, and it won't show respect and honor for him. (Ephesians 6:2) Really, then, this option leads to a no-win situation.

While **Option B** may be the easiest course to take, it's not the wisest. Why? Because "there is a frustrating of plans where there is no confidential

> **TIP**
>
> If you find it difficult just to sit and talk with your parent(s) about a problem, discuss the matter while you are walking, driving, or shopping together.

> **Communicating with your parents isn't always easy, but when you do open up and talk to them, you feel as if a huge weight has been lifted off your mind.** —Devenye

talk." (Proverbs 15:22) To deal successfully with her problems, Leah needs to talk to her dad—and if he's going to be of any help, he needs to know what's going on in her life. Ceasing to talk accomplishes neither.

With **Option C,** however, Leah doesn't let a roadblock become a dead end. Rather, she tries to discuss the subject another time. And if she chooses to write her dad a letter, Leah might feel better right away. Writing the letter may also help her to formulate exactly what she wants to say. When he reads the letter, Leah's dad will learn what she was trying to tell him, which may help him to understand her plight better. Option C thus benefits both Leah *and* her dad.

What other options might Leah have? See if you can think of one, and write it below. Then write down where that option would likely lead.

✎ ....

....

ROADBLOCK 2 Your parents want to talk, but you'd rather not. "There's nothing worse than being hit with questions immediately after a hard day at school," says a girl named Sarah. "I just want to forget about school, but right away my parents start asking: 'How was your day? Were there any problems?'" No doubt Sarah's parents ask such questions with the best of intentions. Still, she laments, "It's hard to talk about school when I'm tired and stressed."

QUESTION: What can Sarah do in this situation? As with the previous example, she has at least three options.

Refuse to talk. Sarah says: "Please, just leave me alone. I don't want to talk right now!"

Option **A**

Go ahead and talk. Despite feeling stressed, Sarah begrudgingly answers her parents' questions.

Option **B**

Delay the "school" talk but *keep the conversation going on another topic.* Sarah suggests that they discuss school at another time, when she knows that she'll be in a better frame of mind. Then she says, with genuine interest: "Tell me about *your* day. How did things go for you?"

Option **C**

Which option do *you* think Sarah should choose? ✎ ....

Again, let's explore each option to see where it would likely lead.

Sarah is stressed and isn't inclined to talk. If she chooses **Option A,** she'll still feel stressed but she'll also feel guilty for blowing up at her parents.—Proverbs 29:11.

Meanwhile, Sarah's parents won't appreciate her outburst—or the silence that follows. They may suspect that Sarah is hiding something. They might try even harder to get her to open up, which, of course, would frustrate her more. In the end, this option leads to a no-win situation.

Option B is obviously a better choice than option A. After all, at least Sarah and her parents are talking. But since the conversation isn't heartfelt, neither Sarah nor her parents are going to get what they want—a relaxed, open discussion.

With **Option C,** however, Sarah will feel better because the "school" talk has been delayed for now. Her parents will appreciate her effort to make conversation, so they'll be happy too. This option likely has the best chance of success because both sides are applying the principle found at Philippians 2:4, which says: "Look out for one another's interests, not just for your own."—*Today's English Version.*

>>> action plan!

The next time I feel I want to stop talking to my parents, I will

....

....

If my parent pushes me to talk about a subject that I am reluctant to discuss, I will say

....

....

What I would like to ask my parent(s) about this subject is

....

....

"I talk straight from my heart and speak sincerely."—Job 33:3, *The Holy Bible in the Language of Today,* by William Beck.

• • • • • • • • •

Avoid Sending Mixed Messages

Remember, the words you say and the message your parents hear do not always match. For example, your parents ask you why you seem to be in a bad mood. You say, "I don't want to talk about it." But your parents hear: "I don't trust you enough to confide in you. I'll talk to my friends about the problem but not to you." Try this exercise by filling in your answers. Imagine that you are facing a difficult problem and your parent offers to help.

If you say: "Don't worry. I can handle it myself."

Your parents may hear: ✎ ....

A better response from you might be: ....

....

The bottom line? Choose your words carefully. Deliver them in a respectful tone of voice. (Colossians 4:6) Think of your parents as your allies, not your enemies. And let's face it: You need all the allies you can get if you are to cope with the challenges you have to deal with.

IN OUR NEXT CHAPTER *What if talking to your parents isn't the problem—it's that each time you talk, you argue?*

WHAT DO YOU THINK?

● **What role does timing play in good communication?—Proverbs 25:11.**

● **Why is talking to your parents worth the effort? —Job 12:12.**

2

Why are we always arguing?

In the opening scenario of this chapter, Rachel contributes to an argument in three ways. Can you identify them? Write your answers below, and then compare them with those found in the box "Answers" on page 20.

....

....

....

It's Wednesday night. Rachel, 17, is done with her chores, and she's ready for some well-earned down-time—finally! She turns on the TV and collapses into her favorite chair.

As if on cue, Mom appears in the doorway, and she doesn't look happy. "Rachel! Why are you wasting your time watching TV when you're supposed to be helping your sister with her homework? You never do as you're told!"

"Here we go again," Rachel mutters, loud enough to be heard.

Mom leans forward. "What did you say, young lady?"

"Nothing, Mom," Rachel says with a sigh, rolling her eyes.

Now Mom is really angry. "Don't use that tone with me!" she says.

"What about the tone you're using with me?" Rachel shoots back.

Downtime is over . . . another argument has begun.

DOES the above scenario seem familiar? Do you and your parents constantly argue? If so, take a moment to analyze the situation. Which topics cause the most conflict? Put a ✔ in the boxes that apply—or fill in your own topic next to "Other."

❏ Attitude   ❏ Chores   ❏ Clothing
❏ Curfew   ❏ Entertainment   ❏ Friends
❏ Opposite sex   ❏ Other ....

Regardless of the topic, arguing leaves you—*and* your parents—feeling awful. Of course, you could just bite your tongue and put on a show of agreeing with everything your parents say. But does God expect you to do that? No. It is true that the Bible tells you to "honor your father and your mother." (Ephesians 6:2, 3) But it also encourages you to develop your "thinking ability" and to use your "power of reason." (Proverbs 1:1-4; Romans 12:1) When you do, it's inevitable that you will have strong convictions, some of which may differ from those of your parents. However, in families that apply Bible principles, parents and youths can communicate peacefully—even when they *don't see eye to eye.*—Colossians 3:13.

How can you express yourself without turning normal conversation into open warfare? It's easy to say: "That's my *parents'* problem. After all, *they're* the ones who are always on my back!" But think: How much control do you have over others, including your parents? Really, the only person you can change is *you.* And the good news is that if you do your part to ease the tension, your parents are more likely to remain calm and hear you out when you have something to say.

So let's see what *you* can do to put a lid on the arguing. Apply the suggestions that follow, and you might amaze your parents—and *yourself*—with your newfound communication skills.

● **Think before you respond.** Don't blurt out the first thing that comes to your mind when you feel that you're under attack. For instance, suppose your mom says: "Why didn't you wash the dishes? You *never* do as you're told!" An impulsive reply might be, "Why are you nagging me?" But use your thinking ability. Try to perceive the feeling *behind* your mom's words. Usually, statements with terms like

DID YOU KNOW . . .

Working to resolve or prevent conflict will make life easier for *you.* In fact, the Bible says that a person "of loving-kindness is *dealing rewardingly with his own soul.*"—Proverbs 11:17.

"Good people think before they answer."
—Proverbs 15:28, *Today's English Version*.

• • • • • • • • •

"always" and "never" are not to be taken literally. They do, however, indicate an underlying emotion. What might it be?

Perhaps your mom is frustrated, feeling that she is burdened with more than her share of the housework. It could be that she merely wants reassurance that she has your support. If that's the case, saying "Why are you nagging me?" will get you nowhere—except maybe into an argument! So instead, why not put your mom at ease? For example, you could say: "I can see you're upset, Mom. I'll do the dishes right away." A caution: Do *not* lace your words with sarcasm. Respond with empathy, and your mom will be more likely to soften and tell you the real problem.*

Below, write a statement that *your* dad or mom might make that could provoke you—if you let it.

✎ ....

Now think of an empathetic response you could use that might address the feeling behind the statement.

....

● **Speak respectfully.** Michelle has learned from experience the importance of *how* she speaks to her mother. "No matter what the issue is," she says, "it always comes back to Mom's not liking my tone of

TIP ✔
When your parents speak to you, turn off your music, set aside your book or magazine, and maintain eye contact with them.

---

* For more information, see Volume 2, Chapter 21.

> *My mom will sometimes say 'I'm sorry' with a hug, and that's nice. Then we can move on. I try to do that too. Putting my pride behind me and sincerely saying 'I'm sorry' goes a long way, although I admit it's not easy.*
> —Lauren

voice." If that's often true in your case, learn to speak quietly and slowly, and avoid rolling your eyes or giving other nonverbal indications of your annoyance. (Proverbs 30:17) If you feel that you're about to lose control, offer a brief, silent prayer. (Nehemiah 2:4) Of course, your objective is not to get divine help to 'get your parent off your back' but to maintain self-control so that you don't add fuel to the fire. —James 1:26.

In the space below, write down some verbal and nonverbal responses *you* are prone to make that you would do well to avoid.

Verbal reactions (what you say):

....

....

Nonverbal reactions (your facial expressions and body language):

....

....

● **Listen.** The Bible states: "You will say the wrong thing if you talk too much." (Proverbs 10:19, *Contemporary English Version*) So make sure that you give your dad or mom a chance to speak and that you give your parent your full attention. Don't interrupt to justify your actions. Just listen. Later, when they've finished talking, you'll have plenty of opportunity to ask questions or explain your view-

Arguing with a parent is like running on a treadmill—you'll expend a lot of energy but won't get anywhere

point. On the other hand, if you dig in your heels and press your viewpoint *now,* you might only make things worse. Even if there's more you'd like to say, right now is probably "a time to keep quiet."—Ecclesiastes 3:7.

● **Be willing to apologize.** It's always appropriate to say "I'm sorry" for anything you did to contribute to a conflict. (Romans 14:19) You can even say you're sorry that

>>> action plan!

The suggestion in this chapter that I need to work on most is

✎ ....

....

I resolve to start applying this suggestion as of (insert date) ....

What I would like to ask my parent(s) about this subject is

....

....

there *is* any conflict. If you find it hard to do this face-to-face, try expressing your feelings in a note. Then 'go the extra mile' by changing any behavior that contributed to the conflict in the first place. (Matthew 5:41) For example, if neglecting a chore has ignited an argument, why not surprise your parents by doing that chore? Even if you dislike the task, wouldn't getting it done be better than facing the consequences when your parents see it's still not done? (Matthew 21:28-31) Think of what you stand to gain by doing your part to reduce the tension between you and your parents.

Successful families have conflicts, but they know how to settle them peaceably. Practice the skills outlined in this chapter, and you may find that you can discuss even difficult topics with your parents—*without* arguing!

IN OUR NEXT CHAPTER *Do you feel that your parents should give you more freedom? If so, what can you do?*

WHAT DO YOU THINK?

- Why do some of your peers prize the ability to argue?

- Why does Jehovah God view an argumentative person as foolish?—Proverbs 20:3.

- What do *you* stand to gain by reducing the tension between yourself and your parents?

3

How can I earn more freedom?

"I wish my parents would let me venture out a little."—Sarah, 18.

"I'm always asking my parents why they don't trust me when I want to go out with a group of friends. Often, they tell me: 'We trust you. We just don't trust your friends.'"—Christine, 18.

LIKE Sarah and Christine, do you yearn for more freedom? To get it, you'll need to gain the trust of your parents. But trust is a lot like money. Earning it is hard, losing it is easy, and no matter how much you're given, it may *never* seem to be enough. "Whenever I want to go out," says 16-year-old Iliana, "my parents bombard me with questions about where I'm going, the people I'm going with, what I'll be doing, and when I'll be back. I know they're my parents, but it irritates me when they question me like that!"

What can you do to get your parents to trust you more and give you more freedom? Before answering that question, let's look at why trust is such a hot-button topic between many parents and youths.

Growing Pains

The Bible acknowledges that "a man will leave his father and his mother." (Genesis 2:24) Of course, the same can be said of a woman. Whether you're a male *or* a female, a vital objective of adolescence is to prepare you for adulthood —the time when you'll be equipped to leave home and perhaps raise a family of your own.*

However, the transition to adulthood isn't like a door that you simply walk through when you reach a certain age. It's more like a stairway that you climb, step-by-step, throughout adolescence. Granted, you and your parents may have conflicting opinions as to just how far you've progressed up that stairway. "I'm 20 years old, and this is still an issue!" says Maria, who feels that she's not trusted when it comes to her choice of friends.

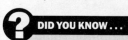

DID YOU KNOW . . .

Unlimited freedom is not a sign of parental love but of parental neglect.

* For more information, see Chapter 7 of this book.

The transition to becoming a trusted adult is like a stairway that you climb, step-by-step, throughout adolescence

"My parents think that I wouldn't have the strength to walk away from a bad situation. I've tried telling them that I have *already* walked away from bad situations, but that's not good enough for them!"

As Maria's comments reveal, the issue of trust can be a source of considerable tension between youths and parents. Is that true in your family? If so, how can you earn greater trust from your parents? And if you've lost their trust because of some unwise actions on your part, what can you do to repair the damage?

Prove Yourself Trustworthy

The apostle Paul wrote to first-century Christians: "Keep proving what you yourselves are." (2 Corinthians 13:5) True, he wasn't primarily addressing adolescents. Still, the principle applies. The degree to which you're accorded freedom often matches the degree to which

> **TIP**
>
> Rather than compare your present restrictions with the freedom an older sibling may have, compare the restrictions you used to have when you were younger with the freedom you have now.

> *When talking to my parents, I am open about my problems and concerns. I think this makes it easier for them to trust me.* —Dianna

you prove yourself trustworthy. Not that you have to be perfect. After all, everyone makes mistakes. (Ecclesiastes 7:20) Overall, though, does your pattern of behavior give your parents reason to withhold their trust?

For example, Paul wrote: "We wish to conduct ourselves honestly in all things." (Hebrews 13:18) Ask yourself, 'What kind of track record do I have when it comes to being up front with my parents about my whereabouts and activities?' Consider the comments of a few youths who have had to take a hard look at themselves in this regard. After you've read their comments, answer the questions listed below.

Lori: "I was secretly e-mailing a boy I liked. My parents found out about it and told me to stop. I promised that I would, but I didn't. This went on for a year. I'd e-mail the boy, my parents would find out, I'd apologize and promise to stop, but then I'd do it again. It got to the point where my parents couldn't trust me with anything!"

Why, do you think, did Lori's parents withhold their trust? ✎ ....

....

If you were Lori's parent, what would you have done, and why? ....

....

How could Lori have behaved more responsibly after her parents first talked to her about the problem?

....

READ MORE ABOUT THIS TOPIC IN VOLUME 2, CHAPTER 22

"You must not use your freedom as an excuse for doing wrong."
—1 Peter 2:16, *Contemporary English Version.*

• • • • • • • • •

Beverly: "My parents didn't trust me when it came to boys, but now I can understand why. I was flirting with a couple of them who were two years older than I was. I was also spending long hours on the phone with them, and at gatherings I'd talk to them and almost no one else. My parents took away my phone for a month, and they wouldn't let me go places where those boys would be."

If you were Beverly's parents, what would you have done, and why? ✎ ....

....

Do you think the restrictions that Beverly's parents placed on her were unreasonable? If so, why? ....

....

What could Beverly have done to restore her parents' trust? ....

....

Regaining Trust

What if, like the youths quoted above, your actions have contributed to your parents' lack of trust? Even if that's the case, be assured that you can turn the tide. But how?

Likely your parents will accord you greater trust and freedom as you build up a record of responsible behavior. Annette came to appreciate that fact. "When you're younger," she says, "you don't fully appreciate the importance of being trusted. Now I feel more responsible, and I feel compelled to act in a way that will help me retain my parents' trust." The lesson? Rather than complain about your parents' lack of trust in you, focus on building up a record of trustworthy behavior. You will likely earn more freedom.

For example, are you dependable in the areas listed below? Put a ✔ in the box next to any traits you need to work on.

- ❏ Keeping my curfew
- ❏ Being punctual
- ❏ Finishing chores
- ❏ Keeping my room clean
- ❏ Using the phone or computer in a balanced way
- ❏ Following through on my promises
- ❏ Being financially responsible
- ❏ Getting out of bed without prodding
- ❏ Speaking the truth
- ❏ Admitting mistakes and apologizing

❏ Other ....

Why not make a personal resolve to *prove* yourself trustworthy in the areas you indicated? Follow the admonition of the Bible: "Put away the old personality which

>>> action plan!

I will be more trustworthy in the following areas:

✎ ....

....

If I lose my parents' trust, I will

....

....

What I would like to ask my parent(s) about this subject is

....

....

conforms to your former course of conduct." (Ephesians 4: 22) "Let your *Yes* mean Yes." (James 5:12) "Speak truth each one of you with his neighbor." (Ephesians 4:25) "Be obedient to your parents in everything." (Colossians 3:20) In time, your advancement *will* be manifest to others, including your parents.—1 Timothy 4:15.

But what if you feel that despite your best efforts, your parents aren't giving you the freedom you deserve? Why not talk over the matter with them? Instead of complaining that *they* need to be more trusting, respectfully ask them what they think *you* need to do to earn their trust. Explain your goals clearly in this regard.

Don't expect your parents to make concessions immediately. No doubt they'll want to make sure that you'll make good on your promises. Use this opportunity to prove yourself trustworthy. In time, your parents may well accord you greater trust and freedom. That was the case with Beverly, quoted earlier. "It's much harder to gain trust than it is to lose it," she says, adding, "I'm gaining trust right now, and it feels good!"

IN OUR NEXT CHAPTER *Have your parents divorced? How can you keep your balance when your world seems to have fallen apart?*

WHAT DO YOU THINK?

- Why might your parents hesitate to give you greater freedom even when you work hard to prove yourself trustworthy?

- How does your ability to communicate with your parents affect their willingness to give you more freedom?

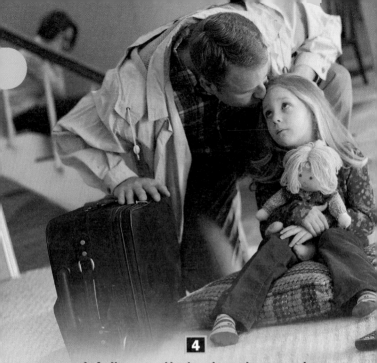

4

Why did dad and mom split up?

"I was home with Mom the day Dad left us. I was only six, so I didn't understand what was going on. I was sitting on the floor watching TV, and I could hear my mom sobbing and begging my dad to stay. He came downstairs with a suitcase, knelt down, gave me a kiss, and said, 'Daddy will always love you.' Then he walked out the door. I didn't see my dad for a long time after that. Since then, I have been afraid that Mom would leave too."—Elaine, 19.

IF YOUR parents divorce, it can seem like the end of the world, a catastrophe that generates enough misery to last forever. It often triggers a wave of shame, anger, anxiety, fear of abandonment, guilt, depression, and profound loss —even a desire for revenge.

If your parents have recently split up, you might be experiencing similar feelings, and no wonder, for our Creator meant for children to be raised by both a father and a mother. (Ephesians 6:1-3) Now you have been deprived of the daily presence of a parent, one you may have deeply loved. "I really looked up to my father and wanted to be with him," says Daniel, whose parents split up when he was seven. "But Mom got custody of us."

Why Parents Break Up

Often, a split-up comes as a surprise to the children because parents have kept their problems well hidden. "I was in shock," says Rachel, who was 15 when her parents divorced. "I always thought that they were in love." Even when parents do squabble, it may still come as a blow when they actually split up!

In many cases the split-up occurs because one parent is guilty of sexual misconduct. Under those circumstances, God does permit the innocent mate to obtain a divorce and be free to marry again. (Matthew 19:9) In other cases, "wrath and screaming and abusive speech" have erupted into violence, causing one parent to fear for his or her physical well-being and that of the children.—Ephesians 4:31.

Admittedly, some couples split up for less compelling reasons. Rather than work out their problems, some selfishly divorce because they claim they are "unhappy" or "no longer in love." This is displeasing to God, who "has hated a divorcing" of that kind. (Malachi 2:16) Jesus implied that some families might be disrupted when one mate becomes a Christian.—Matthew 10:34-36.

Whatever the case, the fact that your parents may have chosen to be silent or to give you only vague answers to your questions regarding the divorce does not mean they do not love you. Wrapped up in their own hurt, your parents may simply find it hard to talk about the divorce. (Proverbs 24:10) They may also find it awkward and embarrassing to admit to their mutual failures.

What You Can Do

Identify your fears. Because divorce can turn your world upside down, you may find yourself worrying about things that you formerly took for granted. Even so, you may be able to shrink your fears to a manageable size by first identifying what they are. Below, put a ✔ next to what you fear most, or identify your own fear by writing it next to "Other."

❏ My other parent will also abandon me.
❏ My family won't have enough money to survive.
❏ The divorce is somehow my fault.
❏ If I marry, my own marriage will fail.
❏ Other ....

Discuss your concerns. King Solomon said that there is "a time to speak." (Ecclesiastes 3:7) So try to discern the right time to discuss with your parents the fears

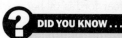

DID YOU KNOW...

Marital unhappiness is not something that you inherit from your parents.

you identified above. Let them know how sad or confused you are. Maybe they will be able to explain what is happening and thus lessen your anxiety. If your parents are unwilling or unable to give you the support

READ MORE ABOUT THIS TOPIC
IN VOLUME 2, CHAPTER 25

• • • • • • • •

you need at the moment, you may be able to confide in a mature friend. Take the initiative to seek out such a person. Just having someone who will listen to you can be a tremendous relief.—Proverbs 17:17.

Above all, you can find a listening ear with your heavenly Father, the "Hearer of prayer." (Psalm 65:2) Pour out your heart to him, "because he cares for you."—1 Peter 5:7.

TIP

If your parents have divorced, one or quite likely both of them have made mistakes. Try to identify those mistakes so that you can avoid repeating them if you choose to marry in the future.—Proverbs 27:12.

What Not to Do

Don't hold a grudge. "My parents were selfish," says Daniel, quoted earlier. "They didn't really think about us and how what they did would affect us." Daniel's feelings are understandable and may be true. But how would you answer the following questions? Write your answers on the line provided.

What harm could come to Daniel if he refused to let go of his anger and resentment? (*Read Proverbs 29:22.*)

....

Although it would be difficult, why might it be good for Daniel to try to forgive his parents for the hurt they have caused him? (*Read Ephesians 4:31, 32.*)

....

How might the basic truth stated at Romans 3:23 help Daniel to view his parents objectively?

....

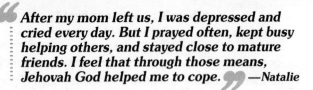

After my mom left us, I was depressed and cried every day. But I prayed often, kept busy helping others, and stayed close to mature friends. I feel that through those means, Jehovah God helped me to cope. —Natalie

Avoid self-destructive behavior. "I was unhappy and depressed after my parents' divorce," recalls Denny. "I started having problems in school and failed one year. After that . . . I became the class clown and got into a lot of fights."

What, do you think, was Denny trying to accomplish by becoming the class clown? ✎ ....

....

Why might he have started getting into a lot of fights?

....

If you have felt the urge to punish your parents by behaving badly, how might the principle at Galatians 6:7

⟫⟫⟫ action plan!

I can express my fears to (write the name of a mature person you would like to talk to)

✎ ....

If I feel an urge to punish my parents by behaving badly, I can control it if I do the following:

....

....

What I would like to ask my parent(s) about this subject is

....

....

Getting over your parents' divorce is like recovering from a broken arm—the process is painful, but you will eventually heal

help you to keep the right perspective? ✎ ....

....

What to Expect in the Future

A literal injury, such as a broken bone, can take weeks or even months to heal completely. Similarly, emotional injuries take time to heal. Some experts feel that the worst of a divorce is over within three years. That may seem like a long time, but remember, a lot has to happen before your life can stabilize.

For one thing, the household routine—disrupted by the divorce—must be reorganized. Time will also pass before your parents are back on their feet emotionally. Only then may they finally be able to give you needed support. However, as your life regains some semblance of regularity, you will begin to feel normal again.

IN OUR NEXT CHAPTER *Feel anxious because your parent remarried? How can you cope?*

WHAT DO YOU THINK?

- Why might your parents be reluctant to talk with you about their divorce?
- Why is it important to remember that divorce is a dispute between your parents—not with you?

5

How can I deal with my parent's remarriage?

YOUR parent might be *so* happy on the day he or she remarries. You, though, might feel anything *but* joy! Why? The remarriage of a parent destroys the hope that your biological parents will ever get back together. On the other hand, the remarriage can be particularly painful if it comes on the heels of the death of a beloved parent.

How did you feel when your parent remarried? Put a ✔ next to any of the descriptions that apply to you.

I felt . . . ✎ ❏ Happy ❏ Insecure ❏ Betrayed
❏ Jealous of my stepparent
❏ Guilty of betrayal because I began
to love my stepparent

That last reaction could be caused by your sense of loyalty to your absent parent. Whatever the reason, the feelings mentioned above might make you vent your emotional pain in destructive ways.

For example, you might constantly make life difficult for your stepparent. You might even try to cause trouble between your parent and your stepparent, hoping to break them up. However, a wise proverb warns: "He who brings trouble on his family will inherit only wind"—that is, he will end up with nothing. (Proverbs 11:29, *New International Version*) You don't have to fall into that trap. You can cope with your emotional turmoil in more productive ways. Consider a few examples.

Challenge 1: Coping With the Authority of a Stepparent

Coming under the authority of a new parent is not easy. When asked to do something, you may be tempted to blurt out, 'You're not my real mother/father!' Such a response may give you a brief surge of satisfaction, but it betrays an immature attitude.

On the other hand, accepting the authority of your stepparent is one way to show that you have heeded the Bible's counsel to "grow up in your thinking." (1 Corinthians 14:20, *The Holy Bible in the Language of Today,* by William Beck) Really, your stepparent performs the duties of a natural parent and deserves your respect.—Proverbs 1:8; Ephesians 6:1-4.

A stepparent's discipline is usually an expression of his or her love and concern for you. (Proverbs 13:24) "My stepdad does discipline us," says Yvonne, 18, "but that's what normal fathers are supposed to do. I feel that if I resent his counsel, then I'm saying that it doesn't matter that he has provided for us materially and spiritually over the years. And that would be ungrateful."

Still, you may have legitimate grounds for complaint. If so, prove yourself to be 'grown up' by doing as Colossians 3:13 urges: "Continue putting up with one another and forgiving one another freely if anyone has a cause for complaint against another."

Below, write two or more good qualities that your step-parent possesses.

✎ ....

....

How could remembering your stepparent's good qualities help you to respect him or her more?

....

Challenge 2: Learning to Share and to Compromise

"My dad ended up remarrying twice," recalls 24-year-old Aaron. "I found it difficult to feel affection for each new stepfamily. At first, they were just strangers, but I was told that I was under compulsion to love them. I found the situation confusing."

You too may face difficult challenges. For example, you might have to relinquish your position as the oldest or the only child. If you are a son, you may for a long time have felt you were the man of the house—a position now occupied by your stepfather. Or you may relate to Yvonne. "My biological dad never paid any attention to Mom," she says, "so I was used to having her all to myself. But when Mom remarried, my stepdad showed her a lot of attention. They spent time together and talked together, and I felt he was stealing her away from me. Eventually, though, I was able to adjust."

Like Yvonne, how can you adjust? "Let your reason-ableness become known to all

? DID YOU KNOW ...

Your stepbrothers or stepsisters may also be having difficulty adjusting to the stepfamily situation.

"Better is the end afterward of a matter than its beginning. Better is one who is patient than one who is haughty in spirit."
—Ecclesiastes 7:8.

• • • • • • • •

men," recommends the Bible. (Philippians 4:5) The original word translated "reasonableness" meant "yielding" and conveyed the attitude of one who did not insist on all his lawful rights. How can you apply that counsel? (1) Avoid dwelling on the past. (Ecclesiastes 7:10) (2) Be willing to share with your stepparent, stepbrothers, and stepsisters. (1 Timothy 6:18) (3) Don't treat them as outsiders.

Which of the above points do you need to work on most? ✎ ....

Challenge 3: Coping With Unequal Treatment

"My stepdad loved his children far more than he did me and my sister," says Tara. "He would buy any food they liked and rent movies they wanted to watch. He'd do anything to please them." Such treatment is hard to bear. What might help? Try to understand why a stepparent may not feel the same way toward a stepchild as he does toward his natural one. Perhaps it is not the blood tie with his natural child but their shared experience in living. After all, you likely feel closer to your natural parent than you do to your stepparent.

 TIP

Living with new siblings of the opposite sex can create moral pressures. So put up a mental block concerning sexual feelings, and make sure that neither your dress nor your conduct is sexually provocative.

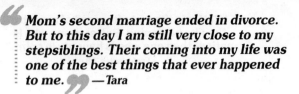

Mom's second marriage ended in divorce. But to this day I am still very close to my stepsiblings. Their coming into my life was one of the best things that ever happened to me. —Tara

There is, however, an important distinction between equal and fair. People have individual personalities and differing needs. So instead of being overly concerned about whether your stepparent is treating you equally, try to see if he or she is striving to meet your needs.

What needs of yours does your stepparent fulfill?

✎ ....

What needs do you feel are not being met?

....

>>> action plan!

I will try to increase my respect for my stepparent by remembering the following good things he or she has done for the family (write down two positive things):

✎ ....

....

If my stepsiblings snub me, I can apply the principle at Romans 12:21 by doing the following:

....

....

What I would like to ask my parent or stepparent about this subject is

....

....

Blending two families together is like mixing water and cement—it takes time and effort, but the end result can be a strong, enduring product

If you feel that some of your needs are not being met, why not respectfully discuss the matter with your stepparent?

Patience Pays Off!

Normally, several years are needed before trust develops to the point where members of a stepfamily feel at ease with one another. Only then may diverse habits and values blend into a workable routine. So be patient! Do not expect that you will experience instant love or that an instant family will result.

When his mother remarried, Thomas was uneasy, to say the least. His mother had four children, and the man she married had three. "We had fights, arguments, disruptions, terrible emotional strains," wrote Thomas. What brought eventual success? "By applying Bible principles, things were resolved."

IN OUR NEXT CHAPTER *What if all your siblings are your natural brothers and sisters but they drive you crazy?*

WHAT DO YOU THINK?

- What fears might your stepparent or stepsiblings have about joining your family?
- Why is it important to take a long-range view of your new family relationships?

6

How can I get along with my siblings?

On a scale of 1 to 5, 1 being "distant" and 5 being "close," how would you rate your relationship with your siblings? 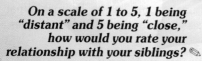 ....

SOME siblings are very close. For example, Felicia, who is 19, says, "My 16-year-old sister, Irena, is one of my best friends." And Carly, 17, says of her 20-year-old brother, Eric: "We get along super well. We never fight."

On the other hand, many have a relationship like that of Lauren and Marla. "We fight about everything," says Lauren. "It doesn't matter how trivial the subject." Or maybe you can relate to what Alice, 12, says about her

14-year-old brother, Dennis: "He gets on my nerves! He barges into my room and 'borrows' things without asking. Dennis is such a child!"

Do you have a sibling who gets on your nerves? Your parents, of course, have the responsibility to maintain order in the household. Sooner or later, though, you will need to learn how to get along with others. You can learn that while at home.

Think about the conflicts you've had with your brother or sister. What do you fight about most? Look at the list below, and put a ✔ next to the type of incident that makes you steam!

- ❏ **Possessions.** My sibling "borrows" items without asking.

- ❏ **Personality clashes.** My sibling acts selfishly or thoughtlessly or tries to run my life.

- ❏ **Privacy.** My sibling enters my room without knocking or reads my e-mails or text messages without asking permission.

- ❏ **Other** ....

⠿ identify the real issue

Want to hone your skills at identifying underlying issues between siblings? If so, read Jesus' parable of the son who left home and wasted his inheritance. (Luke 15:11-32) Look closely at the way the older brother reacted when his younger brother returned home. Then answer the following questions.

What was the **incident** that sparked the older brother's reaction? ✎ ....

....

What do you think was the underlying **issue?**

....

How did the father try to resolve the issue?

....

What did the older brother need to do to resolve the issue?

....

....

Now think of a recent argument you've had with a sibling. Then write your answers next to the questions below.

What was the **incident** that sparked the argument?

....

What do you think might be the underlying **issue?**

....

What ground rules could you agree to that would address this issue and prevent further clashes?

....

If your sibling constantly annoys you—bossing you around or invading your space—it might be hard not to let resentment build. But a Bible proverb says: "The squeezing of the nose is what brings forth blood, and the squeezing out of anger is what brings forth quarreling." (Proverbs 30: 33) If you hold a grudge, it will result in an angry outburst just as surely as squeezing your nose will cause blood to flow. Then the problem will only get worse. (Proverbs 26: 21) How can you prevent an irritation from bursting into a raging argument? A first step is to identify the *real* issue.

Incident or Issue?

Problems between siblings are like pimples. The surface evidence of a pimple is an unsightly sore, but the cause is an underlying infection. Similarly, an ugly clash between siblings is often just the surface evidence of an underlying issue.

You could attempt to treat a pimple by squeezing it. But you would only be dealing with the symptom, and you may leave a scar or aggravate the infection. A better approach is to deal with the infection and thus prevent further outbreaks. It's similar when it comes to problems with siblings. Learn to identify the underlying issue, and you will get past the incident and right to the root of the problem. You'll also be able to apply the advice of wise King Solomon, who wrote: "The insight of a man certainly slows down his anger."—Proverbs 19:11.

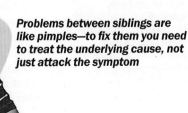

Problems between siblings are like pimples—to fix them you need to treat the underlying cause, not just attack the symptom

For example, Alice, quoted earlier, said about her brother Dennis, "He barges into my room and 'borrows' things without asking." That's the incident. But what do you think is the real issue? Likely, it's related to respect. Alice could deal with the problem by telling Dennis *never* to come into her room or use her things. But that approach treats only the symptom and would likely lead to further conflict. However, if Alice could convince Dennis to respect her privacy and her property, their relationship would no doubt improve.

Learn to Resolve or Avoid Conflicts

Of course, identifying the underlying issues you have with a sibling is only part of the solution. What can you do to resolve an issue and avoid a future confrontation? Try taking the following six steps.

1. Agree to some ground rules. Look back at what you indicated caused conflict between you and your sibling. See if together you can work out some rules that you both agree on and that address the underlying issue. For example, if you clash over possessions, Rule 1 could be: "Always ask before taking an item that belongs to someone else." Rule 2 could be: "Respect a sibling's right to say, 'No, you can't use that item.'" When making these rules, think of Jesus' command: "All things, therefore, that you want men to do to you, you also must likewise do to them." (Matthew 7:12) That way you will make rules that both you and your sibling

DID YOU KNOW...

When you leave home, you will at times be surrounded by people who irritate you —workmates and others who seem rude, insensitive, and selfish. Home is the place to learn how to deal peaceably with such challenges.

"Let your reasonableness become known to all men."—Philippians 4:5.

• • • • • • • • •

can live by. Then check with your parents to make sure that they approve of your rules.—Ephesians 6:1.

2. Abide by the rules yourself. The apostle Paul wrote: "Do you, however, the one teaching someone else, not teach yourself? You, the one preaching 'Do not steal,' do you steal?" (Romans 2:21) How can you apply that principle? If you want your sibling to respect your privacy, for instance, then you likewise need to knock before entering your sibling's room or ask before reading his or her e-mails or text messages.

3. Don't be quick to take offense. Why is that good advice? Because, as a Bible proverb states, "only fools get angry quickly and hold a grudge." (Ecclesiastes 7:9, *Contemporary English Version*) If you are easily offended, your life will be miserable. Yes, your siblings will do or say things that upset you. But ask yourself, 'Have I done something similar to them in the past?' (Matthew 7:1-5) "When I was 13, I thought that I was too cool for everyone," says Jenny, "and that my opinion was the most important and *must* be heard. My little sister is now going through a similar stage. So I try not to get upset over the things she says."

4. Forgive and forget. Serious problems need to be discussed and resolved. But must you call your sibling to account for every mistake he or she makes? Jehovah God

> **TIP**
>
> If you have a brother or a sister whom you find difficult to get along with, take a positive view—that sibling is helping you to develop valuable life skills!

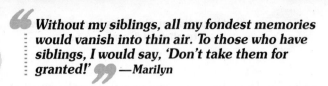

> **Without my siblings, all my fondest memories would vanish into thin air. To those who have siblings, I would say, 'Don't take them for granted!'** —Marilyn

appreciates it when you are willing to "pass over transgression." (Proverbs 19:11) Alison, 19, says: "My sister Rachel and I are usually able to resolve our differences. Both of us are quick to say that we are sorry and then explain what we think was the cause of the clash. Sometimes I'll sleep on it before bringing up a problem. Often, the next morning it's as if the slate is wiped clean, and I don't even have to talk about it."

5. Involve your parents as arbitrators. If you and your sibling can't resolve an important issue, maybe your parents can help you make peace. (Romans 14:19) Remem-

>>> action plan!

Some ground rules I could work out with my sibling(s) are

....

....

I can be less irritating to my sibling(s) if I

....

....

What I would like to ask my parent(s) about this subject is

....

....

ber, though, that the ability to resolve conflict without appealing to your parents is like a mile marker—it's a measure of genuine maturity.

6. Appreciate your siblings' good qualities. Your siblings likely have qualities that you admire. Write down one thing that you appreciate about each of your siblings.

Name	What I appreciate
✎	....
....	....
....	....
....	....

Rather than obsess about your siblings' faults, why not find an opportunity to tell them what it is that you admire about them?—Psalm 130:3; Proverbs 15:23.

The Bible acknowledges that a brother or a sister might not always be the closest companion you will have. (Proverbs 18:24) But you can strengthen your friendship with your siblings if you "continue putting up with one another," even when they give you valid "cause for complaint." (Colossians 3:13) If you do so, your siblings are likely to become less irritating to *you*. And *you* may even annoy *them* less!

IN OUR NEXT CHAPTER *How do you know if you're really ready to leave home?*

WHAT DO YOU THINK?

- Why is it important to see the difference between an incident and the underlying issue?

- What advantages do you see in having siblings?

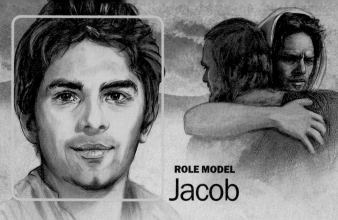

Jacob

Jacob and his brother, Esau, have not spoken in years. In fact, Esau hates Jacob. Even though Jacob has done nothing wrong, he is the one who takes the initiative to heal the rift. He makes concessions. His aim is **not to win an argument** but to win his brother's affection. Jacob doesn't compromise his principles, but neither does he insist on an apology before **making peace** with his brother. —Genesis 25:27-34; 27:30-41; 32:3-22; 33:1-9.

How do you handle disputes with your family members? Sometimes you may feel that you are clearly right and your sibling or parent is clearly wrong. In such situations do you wait for the other person to **make the first move?** Or can you be like Jacob? When Bible principles are not at stake, will you be willing to **make concessions** for the sake of peace? (1 Peter 3:8, 9) Jacob didn't let pride divide his family. He **humbled himself** and won back his brother. Will you do the same with your family members?

7

Am I ready to leave home?

"I sometimes feel that people are looking down on me because I'm 19 and still living at home, like I won't be an adult until I live on my own."—*Katie.*

"I'm nearly 20, and I hate it that I have very little say about how my life is run. I've considered leaving home."—*Fiona.*

LONG before you're ready to leave home, you may begin to feel a desire for independence. That feeling is normal. After all, as discussed in Chapter 3, God's original purpose was for youths to grow up and eventually leave their father and mother and establish their own family unit. (Genesis 2:23, 24; Mark 10:7, 8) But how can you know when you're truly ready to leave home? Consider three important questions you need to answer. The first is . . .

What Are My Motives?

Look at the list below. Number in order of importance the reasons why you want to leave home.

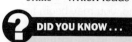 ...... Escape problems at home
...... Gain more freedom
...... Improve my status with my friends
...... Help out a friend who needs a roommate
...... Help with volunteer work in another location
...... Gain experience
...... Ease the financial burden on my parents
...... Other ....

The reasons listed above are not necessarily bad. The question is, What is your motive? For example, if you leave just to escape restrictions, you're likely in for a shock!

Danielle, who left home for a while when she was 20, learned a lot from the experience. She says: "We all have to live with restrictions of some sort. When you're on your own, your work schedule or lack of finances will restrict what you can do." Carmen, who moved overseas for six months, says: "I enjoyed the experience, but I often felt that I had no free time! I had to keep up with the normal housework—cleaning the apartment, fixing things, pulling weeds, washing clothes, scrubbing floors, and so on."

Don't allow others to rush you into a decision. (Proverbs 29:20) Even if you have valid reasons for leaving home, you'll need more than good intentions. You'll need survival skills—which leads to the second question . . .

DID YOU KNOW . . .

Your motive for leaving home can affect how happy you will be after you do so.

Am I Prepared?

Moving out on your own is like hiking in a wilderness. Would you trek into wild country without knowing how to set up a tent, light a fire, cook a meal, or read a map? Not like-

"A man will leave his father and his mother."
—Matthew 19:5.

• • • • • • • •

ly! Yet, many young ones move away from home with few of the skills necessary to run a household.

Wise King Solomon said that "the shrewd one considers his steps." (Proverbs 14:15) To help you determine whether you're prepared to step out on your own, consider the following headings. Place a ✔ next to the skills you already have and an ✘ next to those you need to work on.

❏ **Money management:** "I've never had to make my own payments on anything," says Serena, 19. "I'm afraid of leaving home and having to budget my money." How can you learn to manage money?

A Bible proverb says: "A wise person will listen and take in more instruction." (Proverbs 1:5) So why not ask your parents how much it's likely to cost each week for one person to cover the rent or mortgage, buy food, and run a car or pay other transportation costs? Then have your parents help you learn how to budget your money and pay the bills.*

❏ **Domestic skills:** Brian, 17, says that what he fears most about leaving home is having to

———
* For more information, see Volume 2, Chapter 19.

Moving away from home is like hiking in the wilderness—you need to learn survival skills before you start the journey

> *It's normal to want independence. But if your motive in moving out is just to get away from rules, all that shows is that you're not really ready to move out.* —Aron

do his own washing. How do you know if you're ready to care for yourself? Aron, 20, offers this suggestion: "Try living for a week as if you were on your own. Eat only food that you prepare for yourself, that you buy for yourself at the store, and that you pay for with money you have earned. Wear clothes that you wash and iron. Do all your own housecleaning. And try to get where you need to go by yourself, with no one picking you up or dropping you off." Following that suggestion will do two things for you: It will (1) give you valuable skills and (2) increase your appreciation for the work your parents do.

❏ **Social skills:** Do you get along well with your parents and siblings? If not, you might assume that life will be easier when you move in with a friend. But consider what Eve, 18, says: "Two of my friends moved in together. They were best friends before they shared the apartment, but they just couldn't live with each other. One was neat, the other messy. One was spiritually-minded, the other not so much. It just didn't work!"

What's the solution? Erin, 18, says: "You can learn a lot about how to get along with

TIP

For a time, give your parents the total amount of money it costs to cover your food, lodging, and other expenses. If you're unable or unwilling to pay for your upkeep while at home, you will be poorly prepared to move out on your own.

people while living at home. You learn how to solve problems and make compromises. I've noticed that those who leave home to avoid disagreements with their parents learn to run away from conflicts, not to resolve them."

❑ **Personal spiritual routine:** Some leave home with the specific intention of escaping their parents' religious routine. Others fully intend to maintain a good personal program of Bible study and worship but soon drift into bad habits. How can you avoid 'shipwreck of your faith'?* —1 Timothy 1:19.

Jehovah God wants all of us to prove to ourselves the things we believe. (Romans 12:1, 2) Establish a good personal routine of Bible study and worship, and then stick to it. Why not write your spiritual routine on a calendar and see if you can maintain it for a month without your parents' having to prod you to do so?

Finally, the third question you need to consider is . . .

Where Am I Headed?

Do you want to leave home to get away from problems? Or to break free from parental authority? If so, your focus is on what you're leaving, not on where you're going.

---

* For more information, see Volume 2, Chapters 34 and 35.

>>> action plan!

The goal I would like to achieve by moving away from home is

✎ ....

What I would like to ask my parent(s) about this subject is

....

....

That approach is like trying to drive with your eyes fixed on the rearview mirror—you're so preoccupied with what you're moving away from that you're blind to what is ahead. The lesson? Don't just concentrate on moving *away* from home—have your eyes fixed on a worthwhile goal.

Some young adults among Jehovah's Witnesses have moved so that they can preach in other locations within their country or even overseas. Others move to help with the construction of places of worship or to work at a branch office of Jehovah's Witnesses. Still others feel that they should live by themselves for a time before they get married.*

Whatever your goal may be, think it through. "The plans of the diligent one surely make for advantage," states a Bible proverb, "but everyone that is hasty surely heads for want." (Proverbs 21:5) Listen to your parents' advice. (Proverbs 23:22) Pray about the matter. And as you make up your mind, consider the Bible principles just discussed.

The real question is not Am I ready to leave home? but Am I ready to manage my own household? If the answer to that latter question is yes, then you may well be ready to strike out on your own.

---

* In some cultures it is customary for a child, particularly a daughter, to live at home until married. The Bible does not offer specific counsel on this matter.

WHAT DO YOU THINK?

- **Even if your family life is difficult, how can staying at home for a time benefit you?**

- **While at home, what can you do that will both benefit your family and help you prepare to manage your own household?**

my journal

*Describe a problem that you have recently had with
a family member.*

✎

_____

_____

_____

_____

*Using the suggestions you've read in this section,
write about how you might resolve that problem.*

_____

_____

_____

_____

_____

_____

_____

_____

_____

_____

_____

2 YOUR IDENTITY

8

How can I make good friends?

"If I'm angry, I need someone to vent to. If I'm sad, I want someone to tell me it's going to get better. If I'm happy, I want to share that with someone. To me, friends are a necessity."—Brittany.

IT'S been said that little children need playmates, whereas adolescents need friends. What's the difference?

A *playmate* is someone *who keeps you company.*

A *friend* is someone *who also shares your values.*

Furthermore, the Bible states that "a true companion is loving all the time, and is a brother that is born for when there is distress." (Proverbs 17:17) That's probably describing a deeper kind of friendship than you found as a child at the playground!

Fact: As you progress toward adulthood, you need friends who

1. Have *admirable qualities*
2. Live by *praiseworthy standards*
3. Have a *positive influence* on you

Question: How can you find friends who fit that profile? Let's examine one factor at a time.

Friendship Factor # 1
Admirable Qualities

What you should know. Not everyone who claims to be a friend has what it takes to live up to the label. The Bible even says that "there exist companions disposed to break one another to pieces." (Proverbs 18:24) That might sound extreme. But consider: Have you ever had a "friend" who took advantage of you? What about one who talked behind your back or spread false rumors about you? Such an experience can shatter your trust.* Always remember that when it comes to friends, quality is more important than quantity!

? **DID YOU KNOW . . .**

God is not partial, but he is very selective when it comes to whom he will accept as 'a guest in his tent.' —Psalm 15:1-5.

What you can do. Choose as friends those who have qualities that are worthy of imitation.

"Everyone has such a posi-

---

* Of course, everyone makes mistakes. (Romans 3:23) So when a friend hurts you but then expresses genuine remorse, remember that "love covers a multitude of sins."—1 Peter 4:8.

"There exists a friend sticking closer than a brother."—Proverbs 18:24.

• • • • • • • •

tive view of my friend Fiona. I want to be spoken of in a good way too. I want the same reputation she has. To me, that's admirable."—*Yvette, 17.*

Try this exercise.

1. Read Galatians 5:22, 23.

2. Ask yourself, 'Do my friends reflect qualities that are included in "the fruitage of the spirit"?'

3. List below the names of your closest friends. Next to each name, write the trait that best describes the person.

Name	Trait
....	....
....	....
....	....

Hint: If only negative traits come to mind, it might be time to look for better friends!

Friendship Factor #2
Praiseworthy Standards

What you should know. The more desperate you are for friends, the more likely you will be to settle for the wrong kind. The Bible says: "He that is having dealings with the stupid ones will fare badly." (Prov-

> **TIP** ✓
>
> Live by upright standards, and others who are striving to do the same will be more likely to find you. They will make the best kind of friends!

erbs 13:20) The term "stupid ones" does not refer to people who get bad grades or even who lack intelligence. Rather, it

> *When my parents steered me away from a certain group of friends, I told myself that these were the only ones I wanted to associate with. My parents' advice was good, though, and once I took off my blinders, I realized that there were plenty of better friends available.* —Cole

describes those who turn their back on sound reasoning and instead follow a morally insensible course. That's the kind of friends you can do without!

What you can do. Instead of making friends with just anyone, be discriminating. (Psalm 26:4) No, that's not to say you should be prejudiced. In this context, being discriminating means that you're perceptive enough to "see the distinction between a righteous one and a wicked one, between one serving God and one who has not served him." —Malachi 3:18.

"I'm thankful that my parents helped me to find friends—people my age who are doing well spiritually." —Christopher, 13.

Answer the following questions:

> **When with my friends, am I nervous that they might try to pressure me into doing something I know is wrong?**
>
> ☐ Yes
> ☐ No

> **Am I reluctant to introduce my friends to my parents, fearing that my parents might not approve of them?**
>
> ☐ Yes
> ☐ No

Hint: If you answered yes to the above questions, look for friends who have higher standards—those who set a good example in Christian living.

READ MORE ABOUT THIS TOPIC
IN VOLUME 2, CHAPTER 9

:» try these suggestions

Talk to your parents about friendships. Ask them about the kind of friends they had when they were your age. Do they have regrets about their choice of companions? If so, why? Ask them how you can avoid some of the problems they encountered.

Introduce your friends to your parents. If you're hesitant to do so, ask yourself, *'Why is this the case?'* Is there something about your friends that you know your parents won't approve of? If so, you may need to be more selective when it comes to choosing your friends.

Be a good listener. Show interest in your friends' welfare and concerns.—Philippians 2:4.

Be forgiving. Don't expect perfection. "We all stumble many times."—James 3:2.

Give your friend some space. There's no need to be clingy. Genuine friends will be there when you need them. —Ecclesiastes 4:9, 10.

Friendship Factor #3
Positive Influence

What you should know. The Bible states: "Bad companions ruin good character." (1Corinthians 15:33, *Today's English Version*) A youth named Lauren says: "My schoolmates accepted me as long as I did just what they told me to do. I was lonely, so I decided to act like them just so I'd fit in." Lauren found out that when you conform to others' standards, you are like a pawn on a chessboard, being moved around at *their* whim. You deserve better than that!

What you can do. Cut off ties with those who insist that you change to conform to *their* lifestyle. If you take this step, you may have fewer friends; but you'll feel better about yourself, and you'll open the door to better friendships—the kind that will influence you in a positive way. —Romans 12:2.

"My close friend Clint is levelheaded and empathetic, and as a result, he's been the greatest encouragement to me."—Jason, 21.

Ask yourself the following questions:

> ***Do I change the way I dress, speak, or act in a bad way just to please my friends?***
> ☐ Yes
> ☐ No

> ***Do I find myself going to morally questionable places that I would not frequent if it were not for my friends?***
> ☐ Yes
> ☐ No

⟫⟫⟫ action plan!

To find good friends, I will

....

....

Some who are older than I am with whom I would like to become better acquainted include

....

....

What I would like to ask my parent(s) about this subject is

....

....

When you conform to others' standards just to fit in, you are like a pawn on a chessboard, being moved around at their whim

Hint: If you answered yes to the preceding questions, go to your parents or to another mature adult for advice. If you're one of Jehovah's Witnesses, you could also approach a Christian elder and let him know that you'd like assistance in choosing friends who will have a better influence on you.

IN OUR NEXT CHAPTER *Is a so-called friend—or perhaps your heart—pressuring you to do bad things? Find out how you can resist!*

WHAT DO YOU THINK?

● What qualities would you most value in a friend, and why?

● What qualities do you need to work on to be a better friend?

9

How can I resist temptation?

Karen is at the party for no more than ten minutes when she sees two boys arrive carrying several large paper bags. What's in those bags is no mystery. Earlier, she had overheard the same boys saying that there would be "lots of booze" at this party.

Suddenly, Karen hears a familiar voice behind her. "What are you just standing there for, Miss Boring?" Karen turns to see her friend Jessica clutching two freshly opened bottles of beer. Jessica holds one right in front of Karen's face and says, "Now don't tell me you're too young to have a little fun!"

Karen wants to refuse. But the pressure to accept is more powerful than she expected. Jessica is her friend, and Karen doesn't want to come across as . . . "Miss Boring," as Jessica called her. Besides, Jessica's one of the good girls. And if she's drinking, then what's the big deal? 'It's just a beer,' Karen tells herself. 'It's not like taking drugs or having sex.'

WHEN you're young, temptation comes in many forms. Often, it involves the opposite sex. "The girls at school are aggressive," says 17-year-old Ramon. "They like to touch you and to see how far they can go with you. They won't take no for an answer!" Deanna, also 17, found the same thing to be true. "One boy came up to me and put his arm around me," she says. "I punched him in his arm and said: 'What are you doing? I don't even know you!'"

You too may face temptations, and it might seem as if the pressure just won't let up. Continuous temptation can be like repeated knocking on your door in spite of the "Do Not Disturb" sign. Do you hear that knock more often than you'd like? For example, do any of the following tempt you?

- ❏ Smoking
- ❏ Drinking alcohol
- ❏ Taking drugs
- ❏ Looking at pornography
- ❏ Engaging in sex
- ❏ Other...

If you put a ✔ next to any of the above, don't conclude that you're just not cut out to be a Christian. You *can* learn to control wrong desires and to resist temptation. How? It helps to recognize what's behind temptation. Consider three factors.

1. Imperfection. The inclination to do wrong is common to all imperfect humans. Even the apostle Paul—a mature Christian—candidly admitted: "When I wish to do what is right, what is bad is present with me." (Romans 7: 21) Clearly, even the most upright person will occasionally become aware of "the desire of the flesh and the desire of the eyes." (1 John 2:16) But dwelling on enticements to do wrong only makes matters worse, for the Bible says: "Desire, when it has become fertile, gives birth to sin."—James 1:15.

2. External influences. Temptation is everywhere you look. "At school and at work, people talk about sex all the time," says Trudy. "On TV and in movies, it's always made to seem so glamorous, so exciting. You rarely see the negative consequences!" Trudy knows from experience how powerful the influence of peers and the media can be. "I thought I was in love at 16," she recalls. "My mother sat down with me and told me that if things kept going the way they were, I would end up pregnant. I was horrified that my mom would think such a thing! Two months later, I was pregnant."

3. "The desires incidental to youth." (2 Timothy 2: 22) That phrase can include any desire that is typical of young people, such as the craving for acceptance or the yearning to forge your own identity. Those desires aren't wrong in themselves, but if left unchecked, they can make temptation harder to resist. For example, the longing for your own identity could drive you to turn against the good values you've been taught at home. That's what happened to Steve when he was 17. He says, "I rebelled against my parents and did anything and everything they had taught me *not* to do—all this shortly after being baptized."

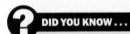

DID YOU KNOW . . .

God foretold that Jesus would prove faithful, but that doesn't mean that Jesus was like a robot, programmed to obey. Rather, Jesus was a free moral agent. His faithfulness was a choice—not a foregone conclusion. That is one reason why he prayed intensely when under trial.—Hebrews 5:7.

How to Resist

Admittedly, the forces described above are powerful. Nevertheless, you *can* resist temptation. How?

READ MORE ABOUT THIS TOPIC IN VOLUME 2, CHAPTER 15

try this!

Take a compass, and position it so that the needle points north. Now place a magnet at the side of the compass. What happens? The needle no longer gives an accurate reading. Instead, it is turned toward the magnet.

Your conscience is like that compass. If properly trained, it will point "north" and help you to make wise decisions. But harmful association, like a magnet, exerts a pull that can distort your moral judgment. The lesson? Try to avoid people and situations that may throw your moral sense off course!
—Proverbs 13:20.

● First, identify the temptation that exerts the strongest pull on you. (You may already have done this on page 65.)

● Next, ask yourself, 'When is this temptation most likely to occur?' Put a ✔ next to one of the following:

✎ ❏ While at school   ❏ When alone
   ❏ While at work   ❏ Other...

Knowing *when* temptation is likely to occur might even help you to avoid it altogether. For example, consider the scenario at the beginning of this chapter. What warning did Karen have that there would be trouble at the gathering she attended?

....

> *What helps me is knowing that I have the most powerful Being in the universe on my side and that I can ask for his help at any time!* — *Christopher*

How could she have avoided the temptation in the first place?

....

● Now that you've identified the temptation and determined when it is likely to occur, you're ready to take action. Your first priority is to figure out how to minimize or eliminate contact with the temptation. Write below what you could do.

....

....

(*Examples: If after school you regularly encounter schoolmates who urge you to smoke with them, perhaps you could alter your route to avoid crossing their path. If you often receive unsolicited Internet pornography, you might consider installing programs to block the source and all similar sites. Also, you could be more specific when selecting the key words you enter in a search engine.*)

✓ TIP

Use the "Peer-Pressure Planner," found on pages 132 and 133 of *Questions Young People Ask—Answers That Work,* Volume 2, to plan responses you can use when someone tries to tempt you into wrongdoing.

Of course, you can't avoid *all* temptations. Sooner or later, you will probably be confronted with a particularly powerful enticement—perhaps when you least expect it. What can you do about that?

When you give in to temptation, you become a slave to your desires

Be Prepared

When Jesus was "being tempted by Satan," his rebuff was immediate. (Mark 1:13) Why? Because he already knew where he stood on the issues that arose. Jesus had already resolved to obey his Father at all times. (John 8:28, 29) He really meant it when he said: "I have come down from heaven to do, not my will, but the will of him that sent me."—John 6:38.

On the next page, write two reasons why you should resist the temptation you most often face and two actions you could take that would help you to resist that temptation.

⟫⟫⟫ action plan!

To build up my determination to resist temptation, I will

✎ ....

....

Some people, places, and circumstances I need to avoid include

....

....

What I would like to ask my parent(s) about this subject is

....

....

"God is faithful, and he will not let you be tempted beyond what you can bear, but along with the temptation he will also make the way out in order for you to be able to endure it."—1 Corinthians 10:13.

• • • • • • • •

Why you should resist:

1 ....

2 ....

Actions that will help you to resist:

1 ....

2 ....

Remember, when you give in to temptation, you become a slave to your desires. (Titus 3:3) Why allow yourself to be controlled by your cravings? Have the maturity to control your urges rather than allow your urges to control you. (Colossians 3:5) And make it a matter of prayer that you continue to do so.—Matthew 6:13.*

* See also Chapters 33 and 34 of this book.

IN OUR NEXT CHAPTER *Feeling sluggish lately? Find out how to improve your health and regain your energy!*

WHAT DO YOU THINK?

● Can perfect creatures be tempted?
—Genesis 6:1-3; John 8:44.

● When you resist temptation, what effect does your faithfulness have on others?
—Proverbs 27:11; 1 Timothy 4:12.

10

Why should I care about my health?

Put a ✔ next to each goal you would like to reach.

❑ Reduce anxiety
❑ Control temper
❑ Feel more confident
❑ Be more alert
❑ Have more energy
❑ Improve complexion
❑ Lose weight

THERE are some things in life that you as a young person don't get to choose—your parents, your siblings, and where you live, to name just a few. Your *health*, however, is a different story. While genetics play a role, your physical condition is often determined by the lifestyle you choose.*

'But I'm too young to worry about my health!' you might say. Do you really think so? Look at the list of goals on page 71. How many did you check off? Believe it or not, good health is a vital key to reaching each one of those goals.

Granted, your feelings might be similar to those of 17-year-old Amber, who says, "No way could I stick to eating whole wheat and low-fat, sugar-free food all the time!" If that's how you feel, don't worry—you don't have to give up sweets completely and jog outrageous distances every week. Really, it may take just a few simple adjustments for you to start looking better, feeling great, and performing at your best. Let's see how some of your peers have done it.

Eat Right—Look Better!

The Bible recommends moderation in our habits. "Don't . . . stuff yourself with food," says Proverbs 23:20. (*Contemporary English Version*) That advice isn't always easy to follow.

"Like many teenagers, I'm always hungry. My parents have likened my stomach to a bottomless pit!" —Andrew, 15.

? DID YOU KNOW . . .

Physical exercise triggers the release of endorphins—chemicals in the brain that can relieve pain and heighten your sense of well-being.

"Because I can't actually see how some foods are harming me now, they don't seem that bad." —Danielle, 19.

Do you need more self-

---

* We acknowledge that many people suffer from health problems or disabilities that are beyond their control. This chapter can help such ones achieve better health within their limitations.

⋙ "I made a lifestyle change"

"I was an overweight teenager, which was something I never wanted to be. I was so unhappy with the way I looked and felt! From time to time, I tried to lose weight with some special diet, but I always gained it back. So when I was 15, I decided enough was enough. I wanted to lose weight the *right* way—a way that I could maintain for the rest of my life. I bought a book that discussed basic nutrition and exercise principles, and I incorporated what I read into my life. I was determined that even if I 'fell off the wagon' or got discouraged, I would not give up. Guess what? It *worked!* Over the course of one year, I lost 60 pounds. I've maintained my desired weight for two years. I never thought it would happen! I think the reason I was successful is that I didn't merely diet—I made a lifestyle change."—Catherine, 18.

control when it comes to your diet? Here's what some of your peers say works for them.

Listen to your stomach. "I used to count calories," says 19-year-old Julia, "but now I just stop eating when I'm full."

Avoid foods that are unwholesome. "By cutting out soda," says Peter, 21, "I lost ten pounds in just a month!"

Adjust bad eating habits. "I try not to go back for seconds," says 19-year-old Erin.

TIP ✔

Get a partner to exercise with. This will give you incentive because you won't want to disappoint the other person.

> *I like the way I feel when I exercise. And when I start to look better because of it, that's a great confidence boost!* —Emily

Secret to Success: Don't skip meals! If you do, you'll feel starved and tend to overeat.

Exercise More—Feel Great!

The Bible says: "Bodily training is beneficial." (1 Timothy 4:8) Yet, many young ones don't seem too eager to exercise.

"You wouldn't believe how many kids failed gym when I was in high school. It was the easiest class, next to lunch!" —Richard, 21.

"Some think, 'Why run around outside in the hot sun until you're sweaty and tired when you can play a video game that allows you to pretend you're someone else doing that?'" —Ruth, 22.

Does the very word "exercise" tire you out? If so, here are three solid payoffs from getting into a good exercise routine.

Payoff #1. Exercise boosts your immune system. "My father always said, 'If you can't find time to exercise, you'd better find time to be sick,'" says 19-year-old Rachel.

Payoff #2. Exercise releases brain chemicals that calm you. "Running is a good release when I have a lot on

Your health is like a car—if you don't maintain it properly, it will break down

my mind," says Emily, 16. "Physically I feel refreshed, and emotionally it's a great relief."

Payoff #3. Exercise can increase your fun. "I love the outdoors," says Ruth, 22, "so my exercise includes hiking, swimming, snowboarding, and biking."

Secret to Success: Devote at least 20 minutes three times a week to a vigorous physical activity *that you enjoy.*

Sleep Better—Perform at Your Best!

The Bible says: "Better is a handful of rest than a double handful of hard work and striving after the wind." (Ecclesiastes 4:6) Without proper sleep, your performance will nosedive!

"If I don't get enough sleep, I'm out of it. I have trouble focusing on anything!"—Rachel, 19.

"At about 2:00 p.m., I get so tired that I could almost fall asleep in the middle of a conversation!"—Kristine, 19.

Do you need more sleep? Here's what some of your peers have done.

▶▶▶ *action plan!*

A reasonable goal I could set with regard to my diet is

✎ ....

A reasonable goal I could set with regard to exercise is

....

I will strive to get an average of .... hours of sleep a night for the next month.

What I would like to ask my parent(s) about this subject is

....

....

"Bodily training is beneficial."—1 Timothy 4:8.

• • • • • • • •

Avoid late nights. "I've been making an effort to get to bed at a decent hour," says 18-year-old Catherine.

Cut out the chatter. "Sometimes friends would call or text me really late," says Richard, 21, "but I've recently learned to end the conversation and just go to sleep."

Aim for consistency. "Lately," says 20-year-old Jennifer, "I'm trying to go to bed and get up at the same time every day."

Secret to Success: Strive to get at least eight hours of sleep each night.

You have everything to gain by taking just a few simple steps to take care of yourself. Remember, having good health will help you to look better, feel great, and perform at your best. Unlike certain things in life, your physical condition is something over which you *do* have a degree of control. "In the end," says 19-year-old Erin, "your health depends on only one person—*you.*"

IN OUR NEXT CHAPTER *Can't see eye-to-eye with your parents when it comes to clothing? Find out how you just might be able to reach an agreement!*

WHAT DO YOU THINK?

- How can taking care of your health affect your self-confidence?

- What is even more important than taking care of your physical health?—1 Timothy 4:8.

11
What can I wear?

Heather is ready to walk out the door, and her parents can't believe their eyes.

"You're wearing that?" her dad blurts out.

"Why not?" Heather replies, sounding astonished. "I'm just going to the mall with friends."

"Not in that outfit!" her mom says.

"But Mom," Heather whines, "this is what all the kids are wearing. And besides, it makes a statement!"

"Well, we don't like what it's stating!" Dad shoots back. "Now go upstairs and change, young lady, or you're not going anywhere!"

77

WARDROBE wars are nothing new. Your parents may have fought similar battles with their parents when they were your age. And back then, they probably felt the same way you feel today! But now they've switched sides, and the issue of what you can wear causes one skirmish after another.

You say: It's comfortable.

They say: It's sloppy.

You say: It's so adorable!

They say: It's so provocative.

You say: It's half price.

They say: It *should* be. . . . Half of it is missing!

Is there any way to declare a cease-fire? Yes! Megan, 23, has learned the secret. "There doesn't have to be an argument," she says. "There can be an agreement." *Agreement?* Does that mean you have to dress like a 40-year-old? Relax! To agree just means that you and your parents discuss your differences and brainstorm other options that they—*and* you—can be happy with. The benefits?

1. You'll look your best, even to your peers.

2. Your parents will be less likely to criticize what you wear.

3. After seeing how responsible you are in this area, your parents may even grant you other freedoms.

So let's get started. Think of a "must-have" outfit that you've spotted online or at the store. The first thing to do is . . .

? DID YOU KNOW . . .

The first impression you make often depends on what you're wearing.

Consider Bible Principles

The Bible says surprisingly little about dress. In fact, you

"Do not let your adornment be that of . . . the wearing of outer garments, but let it be the secret person of the heart."—1 Peter 3:3, 4.

• • • • • • • • •

could read all the Scriptural admonition that directly relates to the subject in just a couple of minutes! In that time, though, you would find solid, valuable guidelines. For example:

● The Bible advises women to adorn themselves "with modesty and soundness of mind."*—1 Timothy 2:9, 10.

The word "modesty" might make you worry. 'Do I have to wear a sack?' you may wonder. Not at all! In this context, modesty means that your clothes show you have self-respect and consideration for others' feelings. (2 Corinthians 6:3) A wide variety of clothing fits those criteria. "It might be challenging," says Danielle, 23, "but you *can* be fashionable without wearing extreme styles."

● The Bible says that when it comes to appearance, you should focus on "the secret person of the heart"—or, as *Today's English Version* renders it, "your true inner self." —1 Peter 3:4.

An immodest outfit may momentarily turn heads, but it's your inner beauty that will win the long-term respect of adults and your peers. Your peers? Yes—even *they* may see the folly of excessive styles. "It's sickening to see

TIP

Avoid styles that highlight sexuality. They make you appear desperate and self-absorbed.

---

* While such Biblical admonition is directed to women, the principles apply to both genders.

Your clothing is like a sign that tells people all about you. What does your "sign" say about you?

the way women practically throw themselves at men by what they wear!" says 16-year-old Brittany. Kay would agree. Describing a former friend, she says: "Everything she wore had 'look-at-me' written all over it. She wanted the attention of the guys, and to get it she would wear the most eye-catching outfits she could find."

Get Your Parents' Input

Stuffing a daring outfit into your backpack and changing into it at school is *not* the way to go. You'll gain more trust from your parents if you're open and honest with them, even in things that you think you *could* get away with. In fact, you'd probably do well to seek out their opinion when you're considering an outfit. (Proverbs 15:22) —Use the "Wardrobe Worksheet" on pages 82 and 83.

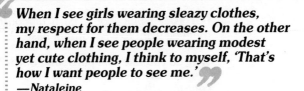

But why would you want to ask for their opinion? Isn't it your parents' job to *stifle* your fashion sense? Not really. True, your dad and mom's perspective may be different from yours, but sometimes that's what you need. "I appreciate my parents' advice," says 17-year-old Nataleine, "because I don't want to walk out of the house embarrassing myself or to be the one that people are talking about negatively because of my appearance."

Besides, let's face it: As long as you're under your parents' roof, you're under their authority. (Colossians

⟩⟩⟩ action plan!

The family member or mature friend I could consult about a clothing item I would like to buy is

✎ ....

The next time I purchase an outfit, I will consider the following factors:

....

....

What I would like to ask my parent(s) about this subject is

....

....

wardrobe worksheet

Instructions: Copy these pages. Ask your parents to fill out the worksheet on the right while you fill out the one on the left. Later, swap worksheets with your parents, and discuss your answers. Are there any surprises? What did each of you learn about the others' perspective that you didn't know before?

for you *Think about a particular outfit that you want to wear or purchase.*

Why do you like this particular outfit? Number the factors below in order of your priority.

- ...... Brand name
- ...... Appeal to the opposite sex
- ...... Acceptability to peers
- ...... Comfort
- ...... Price
- ...... Other ....

My parents' initial reaction to this outfit will probably be

- ❏ "No way!"
- ❏ "Maybe."
- ❏ "No problem."

If they object, the most likely reason would be

- ❏ "It's too provocative."
- ❏ "It's too sloppy."
- ❏ "It's too trendy."
- ❏ "It reflects badly on us as your parents."
- ❏ "It's too expensive."
- ❏ Other ....

can we work

What merit can I see in my parents' view? ....

....

What, if anything, can be done to make the garment acceptable?

....

....

Why, do you think, does your child like this outfit? Number the factors below according to what you think are his or her priorities.

...... Brand name
...... Appeal to the opposite sex
...... Acceptability to peers
...... Comfort
...... Price
...... Other ....

My initial reaction is

❑ "No way!"
❑ "Maybe."
❑ "No problem."

The reason why I might object would be

❑ "It's too provocative."
❑ "It's too sloppy."
❑ "It's too trendy."
❑ "It reflects badly on us as your parents."
❑ "It's too expensive."
❑ Other ....

together on this?

Is our objection to this outfit merely a matter of our personal taste?

❑ Yes ❑ Possibly ❑ No

What, if anything, can be done to make the garment acceptable?

....

....

the decision ....

∴ what about boys?

Bible principles discussed in this chapter apply to boys too. Be modest. Let your secret person of the heart —your true inner self—shine through. When considering an item of clothing, ask yourself: 'What will it say about me? Does that "statement" reflect who I really am?' Remember, clothing is a form of expression. Make sure that your clothes reflect the ideals you believe in!

3:20) Still, once you understand their views—and they, yours—you might be surprised at how often you can come to an agreement. As a result, the wardrobe wars may finally be over!

Fashion Tip: When trying on clothing, think of more than what you see in the mirror. A seemingly modest outfit may change when you sit down or bend over to pick up something. If possible, get the opinion of a parent or a mature friend.

IN OUR NEXT CHAPTER *Are you your own worst enemy? What can you do if you just don't like yourself?*

WHAT DO YOU THINK?

● Why do parents and adolescents often clash over matters of clothing?

● What skills can you acquire by discussing clothing issues with your parents?

12

How can I boost my self-confidence?

	Yes	No
When you look in the mirror, do you like what you see?	☐	☐
Do you feel that you have praiseworthy skills?	☐	☐
Are you able to stand up to peer pressure?	☐	☐
Can you accept valid criticism?	☐	☐
Can you handle unfair remarks others make about you?	☐	☐
Do you feel loved?	☐	☐
Do you take care of your health?	☐	☐
Are you happy for others when they succeed?	☐	☐
Do you generally view yourself as successful?	☐	☐

If you answered no to several of the above questions, it may be that low self-confidence has blinded you to your strengths. This chapter is designed to help you discover them!

MOST youths struggle with uncertainties about their appearance and their abilities, as well as how they measure up to others. Do you fall into that category? If so, you have plenty of company!

"My imperfections cause me to feel down. Usually, I am my own worst critic."—Leticia.

"No matter how pretty or handsome you are, you always come across others who are better-looking."—Haley.

"I get very self-conscious around others. I'm scared that I'll look like a loser."—Rachel.

If you identify with the above statements, don't despair. You *can* get help. Consider three confidence boosters that will enable you to see yourself in a more positive light.

Give of Yourself

Key scripture. "There is more happiness in giving than there is in receiving."—Acts 20:35.

What it means. When you help others, you help yourself. How? "Generosity will be rewarded," states a Bible proverb. "Give a cup of water, and you will receive a cup of water in return." (Proverbs 11:25, *Contemporary English Version*) There's no denying it—your sense of well-being soars when you help others!*

"I think of what I can do for others and try to fill a need for someone in my congregation. Giving love and attention to others makes me feel better."—Breanna.

"The Christian ministry is rewarding because it forces you

? DID YOU KNOW . . .

How you view yourself can affect the way others view you . . . and even treat you.

---

* If you are one of Jehovah's Witnesses, consider the great joy you can gain by sharing the Kingdom message with others.—Isaiah 52:7.

> **"Let each one prove what his own work is, and then he will have cause for exultation in regard to himself alone, and not in comparison with the other person."**—Galatians 6:4.

• • • • • • • • •

to stop thinking about yourself and start thinking about others."—Javon.

Caution: Don't help others solely for the purpose of getting something in return. (Matthew 6:2-4) Giving with the wrong motive falls flat. It is usually seen for just what it is—a false front!—1 Thessalonians 2:5, 6.

Your turn. Think of someone you have helped in the past. Who was that person, and what did you do for him or her? ✎ ....

....

How did you feel afterward?

....

Think of someone else you could help, and write down how you can assist that one.

....

....

Make Friends

Key scripture. "A true companion is loving all the time, and is a brother that is born for when there is distress."—Proverbs 17:17.

What it means. A good friend can be a tremendous support during times of

TIP

Don't tell yourself such things as 'I always fail' and 'I never do anything right.' Such overstatements only keep you down. Instead, acknowledge your shortcomings but also recognize your strengths.

> *A person can be very good-looking and still feel ugly. Or a person can be less attractive and think he or she is the best-looking person around. It's all about attitude.* —Alyssa

adversity. (1 Samuel 18:1; 19:2) Even the thought that someone cares can lift your spirits. (1 Corinthians 16:17, 18) So draw close to those who have a positive influence on you.

"Real friends won't let you stay down."—Donnell.

"Sometimes the most important thing is knowing that someone sincerely cares. That can make you feel valuable." —Heather.

Caution: Make sure your friends bring out the *real* you —not a persona that you create just to fit in. (Proverbs 13: 20; 18:24; 1 Corinthians 15:33) Engaging in unwise acts just to impress others will leave you feeling degraded and used.—Romans 6:21.

Your turn. Below, fill in the name of a friend who might boost *your* self-confidence in a healthy way.

....

Why not make arrangements to spend some time with the person you named above?—Note: The person doesn't have to be in your age group.

Bounce Back From Your Mistakes

Key scripture. "All have sinned and fall short of the glory of God."—Romans 3:23.

What it means. There's no getting around it—you're imperfect. That means there will be times when you will say or even do the wrong thing. (Romans 7:21-23; James 3:2) While you can't avoid making mistakes, you *can* control how you react to them. The Bible says: "Even if good people fall seven times, they will get back up."—Proverbs 24: 16, *CEV.*

"*Sometimes low self-esteem results when we compare our weakness to another person's strength.*"—*Kevin.*

"*Everyone has good and bad qualities. We should be proud of the good and work on the bad.*"—*Lauren.*

Caution: Don't use your imperfection as an excuse to practice sin. (Galatians 5:13) Deliberately engaging in wrongdoing will cut you off from the most important approval you could have—that of Jehovah God!—Hebrews 10:26, 27.

Your turn. Below, write a quality that you would like to improve in.

....

Write today's date next to the quality you noted. Do research on how to improve, and check your progress in one month.

>>> action plan!

When my peers put me down, I will

....

....

When I find that I am noticing only my weaknesses, I will

....

....

What I would like to ask my parent(s) about this subject is

....

....

The value of money does not lessen because it is torn—nor does your value in God's eyes lessen because of imperfection

Your True Value

The Bible says that "God is greater than our hearts." (1 John 3:20) This means, for one thing, that he can see value in you that you may not see in yourself. But do your imperfections change that? Well, imagine that you had a $100 bill with a small tear in it. Would you throw it away or view it as worthless because of that tear? No way! It's still worth $100 —with or without a tear.

It's similar with God's view of your worth. Your flaws don't blind him to your value. He notices and treasures your efforts to please him, no matter how insignificant they may seem to you! Indeed, the Bible assures you that "God is not unrighteous so as to forget your work and the love you showed for his name."—Hebrews 6:10.

IN OUR NEXT CHAPTER *Does intense sadness sometimes overwhelm you? If so, what can you do about it?*

WHAT DO YOU THINK?

- Why might young people be especially prone to lack confidence?
- Why is it important to have a healthy degree of self-respect?

13

How can I stop being so sad?

"When everyone else falls apart, I'm there to fix their problems and make them feel better. But then —and this is the part that few people see—I go home to my room and cry."—Kellie.

"When I'm down, I isolate myself. If I get invited somewhere, I come up with an excuse not to go. I do a good job at hiding my sadness from my family. They think I'm fine."—Rick.

HAVE your thoughts ever been similar to those of Kellie or Rick? If so, don't hastily conclude that there's something wrong with you. The fact is, everyone gets sad now and then. Even faithful men and women of the Bible did. —1 Samuel 1:6-8; Psalm 35:14.

In some cases, you may know why you are sad; in other cases, you may not. "You don't have to be in a horrible situation to feel sad," says 19-year-old Anna. "It can come on at any time, even if your life is trouble free. It's weird, but it happens!"

Regardless of the cause—or even if there doesn't seem to be one—what can you do when sadness holds you in its grip? Try the following:

1. Talk about it. In the midst of his turmoil, Job said: "I will speak in the bitterness of my soul!"—Job 10:1.

Kellie: "The relief I feel after talking to someone is amazing. Finally, someone knows what I'm going through. They can lower the rope and pull me out of the pit—saved at last!"

Suggestion: Below, write the name of a friend in whom you could confide when sadness overwhelms you.

2. Write about it. When sadness clouds your outlook on life, you might want to try putting your thoughts on paper. In his inspired psalms, David sometimes expressed deep sadness. (Psalm 6:6) Writing about such feelings can help you to "safeguard practical wisdom and thinking ability."—Proverbs 3:21.

Heather: "Writing helps me to organize the mental clutter that accumulates from sadness. When you can express your feelings and sort them out, the sadness is less overwhelming."

... to relieve your sadness

event ☹	poor response 😕	better response 🙂		
A teacher makes me feel worthless	I give up trying to succeed in that class	Clue: See Chapter 20 of this book		
A friend ignores me	Spread negative rumors about the person	Clue: See Chapter 10 of Volume 2		
My parents are divorcing	Harbor resentment toward one or both parents	Clue: See Chapter 4 of this book		

How can I stop being so sad? **93**

"Jehovah is near to those that are broken at heart; and those who are crushed in spirit he saves."—Psalm 34:18.

• • • • • • • •

Suggestion: Use the chart on page 93 to help you come up with better responses to trying situations. This will help you to relieve your sadness.

3. Pray about it. The Bible says that if you pray about your concerns, 'the peace of God that excels all thought will guard your heart and your mental powers.'—Philippians 4:6, 7.

Esther: "I was trying to figure out why I felt so down, and I couldn't. I asked Jehovah to help me to be happy. I was sick of being sad when I had no reason to be. I finally broke the cycle. Never underestimate the power of prayer!"

Suggestion: Use Psalm 139:23, 24 as a pattern for your own prayer to Jehovah. Pour out your heart, and ask him to help you identify the root of your sadness.

In addition to the suggestions above, you have a valuable resource in God's Word, the Bible. Filling your mind with upbuilding thoughts that can be gleaned from Bible accounts can have a positive effect on your feelings. (Psalm 1: 1-3) Suggestions for upbuilding Bible reading can be found by considering the "Role Model" pages in each volume of this book. On page 227 of Volume 2, you will even see how the apostle Paul successfully dealt with negative feelings that he sometimes experienced because of his imperfections.

TIP

Describe how you feel when you're sad and what you think may be at the root of your sadness. A month later, read what you wrote. Have your feelings on the matter changed? If so, write down what helped you.

When Sadness Won't Go Away

"On some mornings," says Ryan, "I feel that it would be easier just to stay in bed and avoid having to get up and face another pointless day." Ryan suffers from clinical depression, and he's not alone. Studies suggest that about 1 in 4 youths suffers from some type of depression before reaching adulthood.

With assistance and effort, you can get out of a deep pit of sadness

How can you find out if you suffer from depression? Some symptoms include a pronounced change in mood and behavior, social isolation, diminished interest in almost all activities, a significant

▶▶▶ action plan!

To help lift my spirits, I can engage in the following activities:

✎ ....

....

Associating with the following friends will help me alleviate sadness:

....

....

What I would like to ask my parent(s) about this subject is

....

....

> *When I'm sad, I need to avoid isolating myself.
> Yes, I may need to be alone to process my
> thoughts and maybe have a good cry. But after
> that, I know I need to be around people to get
> my mind off whatever was making me sad.*
> —Christine

change in eating habits and sleeping patterns, and intense feelings of worthlessness or unwarranted guilt.

Of course, nearly everyone has one or more of those symptoms at some time or another. But if symptoms persist for more than a couple of weeks, why not talk to your parents about getting a checkup? A physician can help determine if your sadness has a medical cause.*

If you do suffer from clinical depression, there is nothing to be ashamed of. With treatment, many sufferers have begun to feel better—perhaps the best they have felt in a long time! Whether your sadness is caused by depression or not, remember the comforting words of Psalm 34:18: "Jehovah is near to those that are broken at heart; and those who are crushed in spirit he saves."

---

* When sadness is prolonged, some youths think about ending their life. If you have entertained such thoughts, talk to a trusted adult without delay.—For more information, see Chapter 14 of this book.

IN OUR NEXT CHAPTER *What if your sadness is so overwhelming that you have considered ending your life?*

WHAT DO YOU THINK?

- Are there benefits to shedding tears?
- How can being around others help you cope with sadness?

ROLE MODEL

Job

Job's world is **turned upside down.** First, he loses his means of livelihood. Second, he loses his children in death. Third, he loses his health. All of this happens quickly and **without warning.** In utter despair, Job says: "My soul certainly feels a loathing toward my life." He describes himself as "glutted with dishonor and saturated with affliction." (Job 10:1, 15) Even in the midst of adversity, however, Job refuses to turn his back on his Creator. (Job 2:10) The changes in his life do not change him. Job thus stands as an **example of endurance.**

When confronted with problems, you too might feel a 'loathing toward your life.' Still, like Job, you can show yourself **unchanging in the midst of change,** unwavering in your determination to serve Jehovah God. James wrote: "Look! We pronounce happy those who have endured. You have heard of the endurance of Job and have seen the outcome Jehovah gave, that Jehovah is very tender in affection and merciful." (James 5: 11) He cared for Job, and **he cares for you!**

14

Why not just end it all?

"I AM better off dead than alive." Who said those words? Someone who didn't believe in God? Someone who had left God? Someone whom God had left? None of the above. The speaker was the devout but distraught man Jonah. —Jonah 4:3, *Today's English Version*.

The Bible doesn't say that Jonah was about to take his life. Nevertheless, his desperate plea reveals a sobering fact —at times even a servant of God can be overwhelmed by anguish.—Psalm 34:19.

Some youths feel such intense anguish that they see no reason to continue living. They may feel as did 16-year-old Laura, who states: "For years, I have had recurring bouts of depression. I often think about killing myself." If you know someone who has expressed a desire to end it all—or if you have considered that idea yourself—what can you do? Let's take a closer look at why such a thought might occur.

Behind the Despair

Why would anyone consider taking his or her own life? A number of factors could be involved. For one thing, we live in "critical times hard to deal with," and many adolescents feel the pressures of life with great intensity. (2 Timothy 3:1) Then, too, human imperfection can cause some to harbor deeply negative thoughts about themselves and the world around them. (Romans 7:22-24) Sometimes this is because of mistreatment. In other cases, a medical issue may be involved. Significantly, in one country it is estimated that more than 90 percent of those who did take their life were suffering from some type of mental illness.*

Of course, no one is immune to adversity. Indeed, the Bible says that "all creation keeps on groaning together

---

* It is important to note, however, that most youths who have a mental illness do not commit suicide.

and being in pain together." (Romans 8:22) That includes young people. In fact, youths can be profoundly affected by negative events, such as the following:

● The death of a relative, friend, or pet

● Family conflict

● Academic failure

● The breakup of a romance

● Mistreatment (including physical or sexual abuse)

Admittedly, sooner or later virtually all youths encounter one or more of the situations listed above. Why are some better equipped to ride out the storm than others? Experts

READ MORE ABOUT THIS TOPIC
IN VOLUME 2, CHAPTER 9

say that youths who want to give up the fight feel utterly helpless and hopeless. In other words, such youths see no light on the horizon. They don't really want to *die;* they just want to end the pain.

No Way Out?

You might know someone who wants to end the pain —so much that he or she has expressed a desire to stop living. If that is the case, what can you do?

If a friend is distressed to the point of wanting to die, urge that person to get help. Then, regardless of how he or she feels about it, talk to a responsible adult. Don't worry about ruining your friendship. By reporting the matter, you may well save your friend's life!

But what if you yourself have had thoughts of ending it all? Don't keep your feelings to yourself. Talk to someone —a parent, a friend, or anyone else who cares and who will listen to your concerns and take you seriously. You have nothing to lose—and everything to gain—by talking out your problems.*

Granted, your problems won't disappear just because you're talking them out. But the support of a trusted confidant may be just what you need to put your situation in perspective. It may even help you to work out some practical solutions.

Things Change

When undergoing distress, remember this: No matter how dire a situation may seem, *in time things will change.* At one

---

* Christians who are distressed have an added resource—congregation elders. —James 5:14, 15.

DID YOU KNOW ...

The victims of suicide are not only those who take their life but also the loved ones who are left behind.

Feelings of despair are like storm clouds —in time, they will pass

point, the psalmist David, who was no stranger to adversity, was able to say to God in prayer: "You have changed my mourning into dancing for me."—Psalm 30:11.

David certainly didn't expect the dancing to last forever. He knew from experience that life's problems ebb and flow. Have you noticed that to be true with *your* problems? Some of them may seem overwhelming—at least for now. But be patient. Things change, often for the better. In some cases, problems might be alleviated in ways that you couldn't have predicted. In other cases, you may discover a way of coping that you hadn't considered. The point is, distressing problems will *not* stay the same forever.—2 Corinthians 4:17.

TIP

When you feel down, take a brisk walk. Getting outside and engaging in exercise can produce a sense of calm and well-being.

The Value of Prayer

The most important form of communication you can have is prayer. You can pray as did David: "Search through me, O God, and know my heart. Examine me, and know my disquieting thoughts, and

"Let your petitions be made known to God; and the peace of God that excels all thought will guard your hearts and your mental powers."—Philippians 4:6, 7.

• • • • • • • •

see whether there is in me any painful way, and lead me in the way of time indefinite."—Psalm 139:23, 24.

Prayer is not a mere crutch. It is real communication with your heavenly Father, who wants you to "pour out your heart" to him. (Psalm 62:8) Consider the following basic truths about God:

● He is aware of the circumstances that contribute to your distress.—Psalm 103:14.

● He knows you better than you know yourself. —1 John 3:20.

● "He cares for you."—1 Peter 5:7.

● In his new world, God will "wipe out every tear" from your eyes.—Revelation 21:4.

action plan!

If I feel worthless and unloved, I will reach out to (insert the name of a person you can confide in)

....

One blessing in my life that I can reflect on appreciatively is

....

What I would like to ask my parent(s) about this subject is

....

....

At times, my depression was so intense that I just wanted to die, but now I have my life together again, thanks to persevering in prayer and receiving treatment. —Heidi

When the Problem Is Health Related

As mentioned earlier, suicidal feelings are often rooted in some type of illness. If that's the case with you, do not be ashamed to seek help. Jesus acknowledged that those who are ailing need a physician. (Matthew 9:12) The good news is that many conditions can be treated. And treatment may help you to feel much better!*

The Bible offers a truly comforting promise—that in God's new world, "no resident will say: 'I am sick.'" (Isaiah 33:24) God says that at that time, "the former things will not be called to mind, neither will they come up into the heart." (Isaiah 65:17) In the meantime, do your best to cope with life's challenges, confident that in God's due time, depression will be a thing of the past.—Revelation 21:1-4.

---

* For more information, see Chapter 13 of this book.

IN OUR NEXT CHAPTER *Your parents want to know everything about your life—even some things you'd like to keep to yourself. Can you ever win the battle for some privacy?*

WHAT DO YOU THINK?

- Even severe problems are only temporary. How can reasoning on that fact help you?

- In what way does suicide pass a person's problems on to someone else?

Is it wrong to want some privacy?

Put a ✔ next to your most likely response in each of the following scenarios:

1. You're in your bedroom with the door closed, and your sibling barges in without knocking.

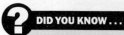

❏ 'No problem. Sometimes I do the same thing to my sibling.'
❏ 'How rude! What if I'd been getting dressed?'

2. You just got home, and now both parents start plying you with questions. "Where did you go? What did you do? Who went along?"

❏ 'No problem. I usually tell them everything anyway.'
❏ 'How frustrating! My parents just don't trust me!'

WHEN you were younger, privacy probably wasn't such a big deal. If your younger sibling barged into your room, you welcomed the company. If your parents asked you a question, you answered without hesitation. Back then, your life was an open book. Now you may wish you could close the cover. "I like it when I can just keep some things to myself," says 14-year-old Corey. Let's look at two areas where trying to get some privacy might pose a challenge.

When You Seek Solitude

There are a number of valid reasons for you to seek out solitude. Perhaps you just want to "rest up a bit." (Mark 6: 31) Or when you want to pray, you may, as Jesus advised his disciples, "go into your private room and, after shutting your door, pray to your Father." (Matthew 6:6; Mark 1:

? DID YOU KNOW ...

The more open you are with your parents, the less suspicious they will be.

35) The problem is, when you shut the door to *your* private room (if you have one), your parents may not think you're praying! And your siblings may not understand when you simply want to be alone.

"Do your utmost to present yourself approved to God, a workman with nothing to be ashamed of."—2 Timothy 2:15.

· · · · · · · · ·

What you can do. Rather than turn the privacy issue into a battle, do the following:

● When it comes to your siblings, try setting a few reasonable ground rules so that you can have some time to yourself. If needed, see if your parents can help in this regard.*

● When it comes to your parents, strive to understand their viewpoint. "At times, my parents check up on me," says 16-year-old Rebekah. "But to be honest, I would check up on my teenager if I were a parent—especially knowing all the temptations young people face today!" Like Rebekah, can you perceive your parents' underlying concerns? —Proverbs 19:11.

● Ask yourself honestly: 'Have I given my parents reason to suspect that I'm up to no good when my door is closed? Have I been so secretive about my personal life that they feel they must resort to covert tactics to learn about me?' If your answer to those questions is no and your parents still seem untrusting, then calmly and respectfully tell them how you feel. *Really listen* to their concerns, and

---

> **TIP**
>
> When talking to your parents about privacy, don't express *complaints.* Express *concerns.* The difference? Complaints focus on what you *think* your parents are doing wrong. *Concerns* help all of you focus on finding solutions.

---

* For more information, see Chapter 6 of this book.

> *Parents don't want anything to happen to you, and at times they may seem to intrude on your privacy. It doesn't seem fair. But honestly, if I were a parent, I would probably do the same thing.* —Alana

make sure there is nothing you are doing that is contributing to the problem.—James 1:19.

When You Make Friends

During adolescence, it's normal for you to form friendships outside your family. It's also normal for your parents to wonder who your friends are and what you're doing when you are with them. But at times you may feel that their concern borders on paranoia. "I just want to have my cell phone and my e-mail without my parents' looking over my shoulder every ten minutes to ask me who I'm talking to," says 16-year-old Amy.

What you can do. Instead of letting your friendships create a barrier between you and your parents, try the following:

● Bring your friends out into the open, and make sure your parents are acquainted with them. After all, you might not like your parents' playing detective, but what choice do they have if your friends are a mystery? Remember, the more your parents know about the people you're spending time with, the more comfortable they're likely to be about your choice of friends.

● Be honest with yourself: Is the issue privacy, or is it secrecy? Brittany, 22, says: "If you're living at home and your parents have a concern, your thought should be, 'What I'm doing isn't bad, so why should I have to hide it?'

Trust is like a paycheck —it must be earned

On the other hand, if you *need* to hide it, then something else is going on."

Privacy and *You*

Now you'll have opportunity to brainstorm some solutions to a specific area of privacy that concerns you. On the lines below, write down your responses to the questions that accompany the following steps:

Step 1: Identify the issue. In what area do you feel that you would like more privacy?

✎ ....

....

>>> action plan!

To gain (or regain) my parents' trust, I will

✎ ....

....

What I would like to ask my parent(s) about this subject is

....

....

Step 2: Consider your parents' viewpoint. What do you think could be their underlying concern?

....

....

....

Step 3: Work at solutions. In what way might you inadvertently be contributing to the problem? What changes could you make regarding your answer above? In what way would you like your parents to address your concerns?

....

....

....

....

Step 4: Talk it out. Describe how you might initiate a discussion with your parents about privacy.

....

....

....

IN OUR NEXT CHAPTER *Has one of your parents fallen asleep in death? If so, where can you find comfort?*

WHAT DO YOU THINK?

- Why do your parents have a right to be inquisitive about your life?

- How might your efforts to build skill in communicating with your parents help you to communicate with other adults later in life?

16

Is it normal to grieve the way I do?

"When Mom died, I felt completely lost and empty. She was the glue that held our family together."—Karyn.

FEW things in life will ever affect you more deeply than the death of a parent. Afterward, you may have to contend with a range of emotions that you have never before experienced. Brian, who was 13 when his father died from a heart attack, says, "The night we found out, all we could do was cry and embrace each other." Natalie, who was ten when

Although this chapter specifically deals with the death of a parent, the principles discussed apply when any family member or close friend passes away.

> *I kept all my feelings locked up inside me. It would have been healthier for me if I had talked more about it. I could have coped better.* —David

her dad died of cancer, recalls: "I didn't know what to feel. So I felt nothing. I was void of emotion."

Death affects each person differently. Indeed, the Bible says that "each one" has "his *own* plague and his *own* pain." (2 Chronicles 6:29) With that in mind, take a moment to think about how your parent's death has affected *you*. Below, describe (1) how you felt when you first found out about your parent's death and (2) how you feel now.*

 1 ....

....

2 ....

....

....

Perhaps your answers reveal that your emotions are, at least to a degree, leveling off. *This is normal.* It does not mean that you have forgotten your parent. On the other hand, you may find that your emotions are still the same or are even more intense. Maybe

* If answering those questions is too difficult at present, you might try to do so at a later time.

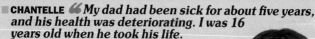

■ **CHANTELLE** 💬 *My dad had been sick for about five years, and his health was deteriorating. I was 16 years old when he took his life.*

Afterward, my mother kept me and my older brother informed of everything that was happening. She even let us help make decisions about the funeral. That made it easier for us. I think that children do not like to feel that things are being kept from them—especially huge things like this. As time went on, I was able to speak openly about my dad's death. Whenever I felt the need to cry, I would just go somewhere or to a friend and cry. My advice is: If you need to talk about it, approach your family and friends. Whatever you have to do to grieve, do it. 💬

■ **LEAH** 💬 *Mom had a massive stroke when I was 19, and she died three years later. After her death, I felt that I had to be strong. The last thing Dad needed was for me to go to pieces.*

When I was growing up, Mom was always there when I was sick or didn't feel good. I remember how her hands felt when she checked me for a fever. Often, I'm painfully reminded of her absence. I tend to bury my feelings, and that's not healthy. So sometimes I look at pictures just to make myself cry. Talking to friends helps too. The Bible promises that those who have died will be resurrected to a paradise earth. *(John 5:28, 29)* When I focus on the hope of seeing my mom again—and when I focus on what I need to do to be there—the stabs of grief lessen. **"**

■ **BETHANY** **"***I wish I could remember telling my dad 'I love you.' I'm sure I did, but I don't remember telling him, and I would like to have that memory. I was only five years old when he died.*

My dad had a stroke in his sleep, and he was rushed off to the hospital. When I woke up the next morning, I found out that he had died. Afterward, talking about my dad both-

ered me, but later I came to enjoy hearing stories about him because that has helped me get to know him better. My advice to any who have lost a parent in death is to savor every moment you had with your parent and to write your memories down so you don't forget them. Then do what you can to build your faith so that you'll be there when your parent is resurrected in God's new world. **"**

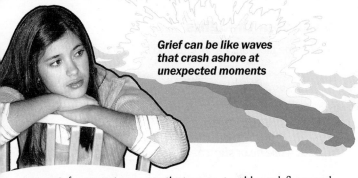

Grief can be like waves that crash ashore at unexpected moments

your grief comes in waves that seem to ebb and flow and then "crash ashore" at unexpected moments. *This too is normal*—even if it occurs years after your parent's death. The question is, How can you cope with your grief—whatever form it takes?

Don't hold back the tears! Crying helps ease the pain of grief. However, you may feel the way Alicia did. She was 19 when her mother passed away. Alicia relates, "I felt that if I showed too much emotion, it would seem to others that I lacked faith." But think: Jesus Christ was a perfect man who had strong faith in God. Yet, he "gave way to tears" over the death of his dear friend Lazarus. (John 11:35) So don't be afraid to let your tears flow. It does *not* mean that you lack faith! Alicia says: "Eventually, I cried. A lot. Every day."*

Address feelings of guilt. "I always went upstairs and kissed my mom good night,"

---

* Don't feel that you *must* cry to manifest your grief. People grieve in different ways. The important thing is this: If you feel tears welling up, realize that it may be "a time to weep."—Ecclesiastes 3:4.

> **TIP** ✓
>
> **Keep a journal. Writing out your thoughts about the parent you lost can be a tremendous aid in coping with grief.**

write your thoughts

List some pleasant memories you have of your parent.

_____

_____

_____

Write down what you wish you could have said to your parent while he or she was still alive.

_____

_____

_____

Imagine that you have a younger sibling who struggles with feelings of guilt over the death of your parent. Write down what you would say to comfort your sibling. (This can also help you to put your own feelings of guilt into perspective.)

_____

_____

List two or three things that you wish you could have known about your deceased dad or mom, and then ask to discuss one of these with your surviving parent.

_____

_____

Read Acts 24:15. How does the hope held out in that verse help you to cope with your parent's death?

_____

_____

says Karyn, who was 13 when her mother died. "There was one time that I didn't do that. The next morning, Mom passed away. As unrealistic as it sounds, I feel guilty for not having seen her that last night—and for the chain of events that occurred the next morning. My dad left on a business trip and wanted me and my sister to look in on Mom. But we slept late. When I went into the bedroom, Mom wasn't breathing. I felt terrible, because she was OK when Dad left!"

Like Karyn, perhaps you feel a measure of guilt for things you neglected to do. You might even torture yourself with "if onlys." 'If only I had urged Dad to see a doctor.' 'If only I had checked on Mom earlier.' If such thoughts plague you, remember this: It's normal to feel regret over things you wish you had done differently. The fact is, you *would* have done things differently had you known what would happen. But you did not know. Therefore, guilt is inappropriate. *You are not responsible for your parent's death!**

Communicate your feelings. Proverbs 12:25 states: "Kind words will cheer you up." (*Today's English Version*) Keeping your feelings bottled up inside may make it difficult

---

* If such thoughts continue to plague you, share your feelings with your surviving parent or another adult. In time, you will acquire a more balanced outlook.

>>> **action plan!**

When I feel overwhelmed with grief, I will

....

....

What I would like to ask my surviving parent about this subject is

....

....

> **"[God] will wipe out every tear from their eyes, and death will be no more, neither will mourning nor outcry nor pain be anymore. The former things have passed away."**
> —Revelation 21:4.

• • • • • • • • •

for you to deal with your grief. On the other hand, discussing your feelings with someone you trust will open the way for you to receive "kind words" of encouragement when you need them most.

Talk to God. Likely, you will feel much better after you "pour out your heart" to Jehovah God in prayer. (Psalm 62:8) This is not simply a 'feel-good therapy.' In prayer, you are appealing to "the God of all comfort, who comforts us in all our tribulation." (2 Corinthians 1:3, 4) One way that God provides comfort is through his Word, the Bible. (Romans 15:4) Why not keep handy a list of scriptures that are comforting to you?*

Grieving is not an overnight process. But the Bible can provide comfort, for it assures us that in the new world that God promises to bring about, "death will be no more, neither will mourning nor outcry nor pain be anymore." (Revelation 21:3, 4) You too may find that meditating on such promises will help you cope with the loss of your parent.

---

* Some have been comforted by the following scriptures: Psalm 34:18; 102:17; 147:3; Isaiah 25:8; John 5:28, 29.

WHAT DO YOU THINK?

- Why is it good to reflect on pleasant memories you have of the parent you lost in death?

- Why can writing out your thoughts help you to cope with grief?

my journal

Write down three traits that you value in a true friend. Then write about what you can do to acquire or improve those same traits in yourself.

_____

_____

_____

_____

_____

_____

_____

_____

_____

_____

_____

_____

_____

_____

_____

_____

_____

_____

3 IN AND OUT OF CLASS

17

Why am I afraid to share my faith at school?

"There have been some great opportunities to talk about my beliefs at school. But I let them pass."— Kaleb.

"Our teacher asked the class what we thought about evolution. I knew this was a perfect chance to share my faith. But I completely froze and said nothing. Afterward, I felt really bad."— Jasmine.

IF YOU are a Christian youth, perhaps you can relate to the experiences of Kaleb and Jasmine. Like them, you may love the Bible-based truths you have learned. You may even want to share them with others. Still, you might *dread* the thought of speaking up. But you can develop more courage. How? Take the following steps:

1. Define your fears. When you think about sharing your faith, it's easy to imagine the worst-case scenario! Sometimes, though, you can shrink your fears simply by putting them into words.

Complete the following sentence:

● This is what I fear might happen if I talk about my beliefs at school: ✎ ....

....

If it's any comfort, your fears may be a lot like those of other Christian youths. For instance, 14-year-old Christopher admits, "I'm afraid kids will make fun of me and tell everyone I'm weird." And Kaleb, quoted at the outset, says, "I was worried someone would ask a question and I wouldn't know the answer."

2. Accept the challenge. Are your fears completely unfounded? Not necessarily, as 20-year-old Ashley recalls. "Some kids pretended they were interested in my beliefs," she says. "But later they turned my words against me and teased me in front of others." Nicole, 17, had this experience: "A boy compared a verse in his Bible with the same verse in mine, and the wording was different. He said

? DID YOU KNOW ...

Some of your classmates may admire you for sticking to the Bible's moral standards, but they may be too shy to ask about your religious beliefs.

"Always [be] ready to make a defense before everyone that demands of you a reason for the hope in you, but doing so together with a mild temper and deep respect."—1 Peter 3:15.

• • • • • • • • •

that my Bible had been changed. I was stunned! I didn't know what to say."*

Situations like these can seem pretty scary! But instead of running away, accept such challenges for what they are —a normal part of your life as a Christian. (2 Timothy 3: 12) "Jesus said his followers would be persecuted," says 13-year-old Matthew, "so we can't expect everyone to like us for our beliefs."—John 15:20.

3. Think of the benefits. Can any good come out of a seemingly bad experience? Amber, 21, thinks so. "It's hard to explain your faith to people who don't respect the Bible," she says, "but it helps you to understand your own position better."—Romans 12:2.

Look again at the scenario you described in Step 1. Think of at least two good things that could come out of that situation, and write them below.

1 ....

2 ....

Hint: How might making known your faith lead to a decrease in the peer pressure you face? How will speaking up affect your self-confidence?

> **TIP** ✓
>
> **Rather than tell your classmates what they should or should not believe, state confidently what you believe and why you feel that your conclusions are reasonable.**

---

* Bible translations use different wording. However, some are more faithful to the original languages in which the Bible was written.

- **"What are your plans for the summer?"**
  [After response, mention your spiritual plans, such as attending a convention or expanding your ministry.]

- Mention a news item, and then ask: **"Did you hear about that? What do you think of it?"**

- **"Do you think that the world's financial situation** [or another problem] **is likely to improve?** [Allow for response.] **Why do you feel that way?"**

- **"Do you belong to a religion?"**

- **"Where do you see yourself five years from now?"** [After response, share your spiritual goals.]

Your feelings for Jehovah God? His feelings for you? —Proverbs 23:15.

4. **Be prepared.** "The heart of the righteous one meditates so as to answer," says Proverbs 15:28. Besides meditating on what you'll say, try to anticipate questions others may ask. Research those topics, and plan out answers you feel comfortable giving.—See the chart "Plan Your Response," on page 127.

5. **Get started.** Once you're ready to talk about your beliefs, how should you start? You have options. In a sense, sharing your faith is like swimming: Some people ease their way into the water; others jump right in. Likewise, you could start the conversation on a nonreligious subject and gradually test the water, so to speak. But if you find yourself worrying too much about what might go wrong, your best option may be to 'jump right in.' (Luke

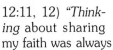

Sharing your faith is like swimming. You can choose to start slowly—or just take the plunge!

12:11, 12) *"Thinking* about sharing my faith was always harder than actually *doing* it," says 17-year-old Andrew. "Once a conversation was started, it was much easier than I thought it would be!"*

6. Be sensible. "Sensible people always think before they act," wrote Solomon. (Proverbs 13:16, *Today's English Version*) Just as you wouldn't dive into shallow waters, be careful not to jump into pointless arguments. Remember, there's a time to speak and a time to keep quiet.

---

* See the box "Conversation Starters," on the previous page.

⟫⟫ action plan!

A classmate I could talk to about my beliefs is [write the name of at least one person]

✎ ....

....

The topic I think will interest that person most is

....

What I would like to ask my parent(s) about this subject is

....

....

> *When I was younger, I didn't want to be different from other kids. But then I began to appreciate how my faith contributes to a better quality of life. That realization boosted my confidence—it made me feel proud of what I believe.* —Jason

(Ecclesiastes 3:1, 7) At times, even Jesus refused to answer questions.—Matthew 26:62, 63.

If you do choose to reply, you might keep it brief and be discreet. For example, if a classmate taunts, 'Why don't you smoke cigarettes?' you could simply say, 'Because I'm not into body pollution!' Depending on the response, you can decide whether or not to explain your beliefs further.

The six steps outlined in this chapter can help you to be "ready to make a defense" of your faith. (1 Peter 3:15) Of course, being ready doesn't mean that you'll never feel nervous. But Alana, 18, observes: "When you explain your beliefs *despite being scared*, it makes you feel as if you've accomplished something—you've overcome your fear and taken the risk that it might not go well. And if it *does* go well, you'll feel even better! You'll be glad you had the courage to speak up."

IN OUR NEXT CHAPTER *Stressed out at school? Find out how you can cope.*

WHAT DO YOU THINK?

- What might be an underlying reason why schoolmates ridicule your religious beliefs?
- If you decide to talk about your beliefs, why is it important that you speak confidently?

Plan your response

Suggestion: Discuss this chart with your parents and with fellow Christian youths. Complete the chart. Then see if you can think of other questions your classmates may ask, and plan responses that you feel comfortable with.

...copy this!

	question	answer	next question	answer
neutrality	Why don't you salute the flag? Don't you love your country?	I respect the land I live in, but I don't worship it.	So you wouldn't fight for your country?	No, and millions of Jehovah's Witnesses in other lands wouldn't fight *against* this country either.
blood	Why won't you accept blood transfusions?	I accept safe transfusions—the kind that don't carry the risk of AIDS or hepatitis. But the Bible says to abstain from blood, so that's where I draw the line.	But what if you were going to die unless you took blood? Wouldn't God forgive you? 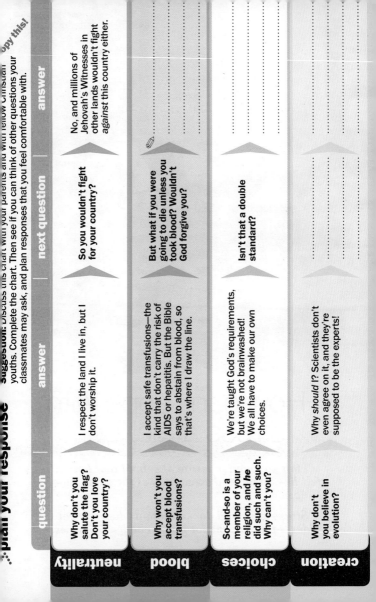	
choices	So-and-so is a member of your religion, and *he* did such and such. Why can't you?	We're taught God's requirements, but we're not brainwashed! We all have to make our own choices.	Isn't that a double standard?	
creation	Why don't you believe in evolution?	Why *should* I? Scientists don't even agree on it, and they're supposed to be the experts!		

18

How can I cope with stress at school?

"I felt so much pressure at school that I often felt like crying and screaming at the same time." — Sharon.

"Stress at school doesn't let up when you get older—the reasons for it just change." — James.

DO YOU feel that your parents just don't understand how much stress you're under at school? They might tell you that you don't have a mortgage to pay off, a family to feed, or an employer to please. Likely, though, you feel that at school you face as much pressure as your parents do—or *more*.

Just getting to and from school can be stressful. "Fights often broke out on the school bus," says Tara, who lives in the United States. "The driver would stop, and everyone would have to get off. We would all be delayed by half an hour or more."

Does the stress let up once you arrive at school? Hardly! Perhaps you face the following:

● **Teacher-induced stress.**

"My teachers want me to excel and get the best grades possible, and I feel pressure to gain their approval." —Sandra.

"Teachers push students to excel academically, especially if the student has some ability."—April.

"Even if you have worthwhile goals for your life, some teachers make you feel like dirt if you don't pursue the academic goals that they think you should."*—Naomi.

How are you affected by teacher-induced stress?

✎ ....

....

● **Peer-induced stress.**

"In high school, kids have more freedom and they're more rebellious. If you don't join them, they think you're not cool."—Kevin.

"On a daily basis, I face the temptation to become involved in drinking and sex. Sometimes it's hard to resist the desire to join in."—Aaron.

---

* For more information, see Chapter 20 of this book.

"Now that I'm 12, the biggest stress for me is the pressure to date. Everyone at school says, 'How long are you going to stay single?'"—Alexandria.

"I was pressured to go out with a boy. When I refused, I was labeled a lesbian. And that was when I was just ten years old!"—Christa.

How are you affected by peer-induced stress?

....

....

● **Other stress factors.** Put a ✔ next to the one that affects you most—or write in the one that does.

❏ Upcoming tests
❏ Homework
❏ Parents' high expectations
❏ Living up to your own high expectations
❏ Bullying or sexual harassment
❏ Other ....

Four Steps to Less Stress

Realistically, you can't expect to make it through school without having to deal with some kind of stress. Granted, too much stress can be oppressive. Wise King Solomon wrote: "Mere oppression may make a wise one act crazy." (Ecclesiastes 7:7) But you need not let that happen to you. The key is learning how to manage stress effectively.

Coping with stress is like lifting weights. To be successful, a weight lifter must prepare properly beforehand. He doesn't load the bar with more

? DID YOU KNOW ...

Getting enough sleep each night—at least eight hours—not only helps you cope with stress but also improves your memory.

Just as lifting weights correctly can make you physically stronger, dealing with stress correctly can make you emotionally stronger

than he can carry, and he picks up the weights correctly. If he takes such steps, he builds strong muscles without damaging his body. On the other hand, if he fails to take these steps, he can tear a muscle or even break a bone.

Similarly, you can manage the stresses that you encounter and successfully accomplish the work you need to do without causing damage to yourself. How? Take the following steps:

1. Identify the specific causes. "When you see trouble coming, don't be stupid and walk right into it—be smart and hide," states a wise proverb. (Proverbs 22:3, *Contemporary English Version*) But you can't hide from oppressive stress unless you first identify the most likely cause. So look back at what you placed a ✔ next to earlier. Which stress factor affects you the most right now?

2. Do research. For example, if a heavy load of homework is stressing you out, research the suggestions found in Chapter 13 of Volume 2. If you feel pressured to engage in sexual misconduct with a classmate, you'll also find helpful advice in Chapters 2, 5, and 15 of that volume.

3. Don't procrastinate. Few problems will disappear if you ignore them. Instead, they usually become worse, thus increasing your stress. Once you've decided how you will deal with a particular stress, don't delay. Do it right away.

> *Every day my dad would say a prayer with me before he dropped me off at school. It always made me feel safe.* —Liz

For instance, if you're one of Jehovah's Witnesses and are thus trying to live by the Bible's moral standards, identify yourself as such as soon as possible. Doing so can lessen your stress. Marchet, 20, says: "Right at the start of each school year, I initiated a conversation about some subject that I knew would give me a chance to explain my Bible-based standards. I found that the longer I waited to identify myself as a Witness, the harder it became. It really helped when I made my stand known and then lived up to my ideals throughout the year."

TIP

Divide the problems that cause you stress into two categories —those you can do something about and those you cannot control. First, work on the problems you *can* do something about. Then, when all of those problems are gone—*if that day ever comes*—you'll have plenty of time left to think about the problems you cannot fix.

4. Ask for help. Even the strongest weight lifter has his limits. You do too. But you don't have to carry the burden by yourself. (Galatians 6:2) Why not talk to your parents

>>> action plan!

To help me cope with stress, I resolve that when possible I will go to bed at ✎ ....

What I would like to ask my parent(s) about this subject is

....

....

"Throw all your anxiety upon [God], because he cares for you."—1 Peter 5:7.

• • • • • • • • •

or another mature Christian? Show them the answers that you wrote earlier in this chapter. Ask for their suggestions.

Good Stress?

You might find it hard to believe, but the fact that you feel some stress is actually a good thing. Why? It indicates that you're diligent and that your conscience hasn't become lazy. Note how the Bible describes an individual who seemed to feel no stress at all: "How long will you lie there doing nothing at all? When are you going to get up and stop sleeping? Sleep a little. Doze a little. Fold your hands and twiddle your thumbs. Suddenly, everything is gone, as though it had been taken by an armed robber."—Proverbs 6:9-11, *Contemporary English Version.*

Heidi, 16, sums up the matter well. She says: "School may seem like a really bad place, but the pressures you face there are the same ones you'll face in the workforce." True, coping with stress isn't easy. But if managed properly, stress won't harm you. In fact, it can make you a stronger person.

IN OUR NEXT CHAPTER *Is quitting school the answer to your problems?*

WHAT DO YOU THINK?

- Why would being a perfectionist only increase your stress?
- Whom could you talk to if you were overwhelmed by stress?

19

Should I quit school?

At what grade do you think you should leave school? ✎ ....

At what grade do your parents want you to leave? ....

DO THE two answers above match? Even if they do and you're still in school, you may have days when you wish you could quit. Can you relate to the following comments?

"Sometimes I'd get so stressed out that I didn't want to get out of bed. I'd think, 'Why do I need to go to school and learn things that I'm never going to use?'"—Rachel.

"Many times I've been tired of school and just wanted to drop out and get a job. I've felt that school was doing me no

good and that I would rather be getting paid for my time."
—John.

"I went to an inner-city high school and had trouble fitting in. I didn't have any difficulty with the schoolwork, but I was an outcast and spent a lot of time alone. Not even the other outcasts would talk to me! I was very tempted just to quit."—Ryan.

"I had up to four hours of homework a night! I became so bogged down with assignments, projects, and tests—all back-to-back—that I felt I couldn't handle it and wanted out."—Cindy.

"We've had a bomb threat, three suicide attempts, one actual suicide, and gang violence. Sometimes it just got to be too much, and I wanted to leave!"—Rose.

Have you faced similar challenges? If so, what situation has made you want to quit school?

✎
....

Maybe you are now seriously planning on quitting. How, though, can you tell if you're leaving because it's time to do so or because you are just sick of school and want out? To answer that, we first need to define what it means to quit school.

Leaving or Quitting?

How would you describe the difference between leaving school and quitting school?

....

....

Did you know that in some countries it's normal for a youth to graduate after between five and eight years of instruction? In other lands, students are expected to stay in school for at least ten years. So, there is no set age or grade that applies to everyone equally around the world.

In addition, some countries or states may allow a student to take some or all of his or her classes from home, without going to a regular school. Students who are home-schooled—with their parents' permission and cooperation, of course—are not quitting.

However, if you're thinking of ending your school career *before* you graduate—either regular school or school at home—you need to consider the following questions:

What does the law require? As mentioned, laws governing the amount of schooling a student must have differ from place to place. What is the minimum schooling that the law in your area requires? Have you reached that stage yet? If you ignore the Bible's counsel to be "in subjection to the superior authorities" and you leave before that grade, you are quitting.—Romans 13:1.

Have I achieved my educational goals? What are the goals that you want your education to help you achieve? Not sure? You need to know! Otherwise, you're like a train passenger who has no idea where he wants to go. So sit down with your parents, and fill in the worksheet "My Educational Goals," found on page 139. Doing so will assist you to stay focused and will help you and your parents to plan how long you should stay in school.—Proverbs 21:5.

Your teachers and others will no doubt give you advice on how much schooling you should have. Ultimately, though, your parents have the authority to make the final decision. (Proverbs 1:8; Colossians 3:20) If you leave before you reach the educational

? DID YOU KNOW . . .

Youths who skip classes are more likely to end up dropping out of school.

• • • • • • • • •

goals that you and your parents decide upon, you are quitting.

What are my motives for dropping out? Beware of fooling yourself. (Jeremiah 17:9) It's a human tendency to give noble reasons for selfish actions.—James 1:22.

Write here the honorable reasons you might have for ending your school career before you graduate.

....
....

Write here some selfish reasons for quitting.

....
....

What honorable reasons did you write? A couple of possibilities might be to help support your family financially or to engage in volunteer work. Selfish reasons might be to avoid tests or to escape homework. The challenge is to discern which is your primary motivation—and if it is honorable or selfish.

Look again at the list you wrote above, and honestly rate from 1 to 5 the reasons why you want to quit school (1 indicating less important, 5 most important). If you drop out just to escape problems, you are likely in for a shock.

What's Wrong With Quitting?

Quitting school is like jumping off a train before you reach your destination. The train may be uncomfortable, and the passengers unfriendly. But if you leap from the train, you obviously will not reach your destination and will

Quitting school is like jumping off a train before you reach your destination

likely cause yourself serious injury. Similarly, if you quit school, you may not reach your educational goals and you will cause yourself both immediate and long-term problems, such as the following:

Immediate problems:

You will likely find it more difficult to get a job. And if you do get one, it will probably be lower paying than one you might have obtained if you had completed your schooling. To support a basic standard of living, you may then have to work longer hours in surroundings that will likely be even less pleasant than your current school environment.

Long-term challenges: Research shows that those who drop out of school are more likely to have poorer health, to end up in prison, and to have to rely on social welfare programs.

Of course, completing school is no guarantee that you'll avoid those problems. But why unnecessarily handicap yourself by dropping out?

Benefits of Not Quitting

If you've just failed a test or had a difficult day at school, you might want to give up —any future problems may seem insignificant compared with your present grind. But

TIP

If you are struggling to cope with the school environment, see if you can enroll in accelerated programs that will allow you to graduate earlier.

∴ my educational goals

A primary function of education is to prepare you to find a job that will help you support yourself and provide for any family you may eventually have. (2 Thessalonians 3:10, 12) Have you decided what kind of job you want and how your time at school can help you prepare for it? To assist you to see if your education is leading you in the right direction, answer the following questions:

What are my strengths? (For instance, do you interact well with people? Do you enjoy working with your hands or creating or fixing things? Are you good at analyzing and solving problems?)

✎ ....

What jobs would allow me to use my strengths?

....

What employment opportunities are available where I live?

....

What classes am I now taking that prepare me for the job market?

....

What educational options do I currently have that would help me reach my goals more efficiently?

....

Remember, your goal is to graduate with an education that you can use. So don't go to the other extreme and be a perennial student—one who stays "on the train" indefinitely just to hide from the responsibilities of adulthood.*

---

* For more information, see Volume 2, Chapter 38.

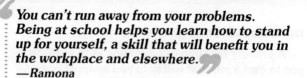

You can't run away from your problems. Being at school helps you learn how to stand up for yourself, a skill that will benefit you in the workplace and elsewhere.
—*Ramona*

before you take the "easy" option, consider what the students quoted at the outset of this chapter say about how they benefited because they did not drop out.

"I've learned endurance, to be mentally tough. I've also learned that if you want to have a good time doing something, you have to make it happen. Along the way, I've improved my art skills, which I will use when I graduate." —*Rachel.*

"I now know that if I work hard, I can reach my goals. I'm taking a very practical technical training course in high school that will help qualify me for my preferred job as a press mechanic."—*John.*

⟫⟫ action plan!

If I am having difficulty with a subject, rather than quitting I will

....

....

If fatigue is making me feel like quitting school, I will be able to cope if I

....

....

What I would like to ask my parent(s) about this subject is

....

....

"Because I persisted, I have mastered the fundamentals of reading and writing. School has taught me how to benefit from criticism and how to express myself clearly and logically—skills that are useful in my Christian ministry."—Ryan.

"School has improved my problem-solving ability, whether in the classroom or elsewhere. Figuring out ways to deal with academic, social, and physical challenges has really helped me to mature."—Cindy.

"School has helped prepare me for the challenges of the work environment. Also, I faced many situations that forced me to examine the reasons for my faith, so being at school has strengthened my religious convictions."—Rose.

Wise King Solomon wrote: "Better is the end afterward of a matter than its beginning. Better is one who is patient than one who is haughty in spirit." (Ecclesiastes 7:8) So rather than quit, patiently work through the problems you face at school. If you do, you will find that the end afterward will be much better for you.

IN OUR NEXT CHAPTER *What if one reason you hate school is that you can't get along with your teacher?*

WHAT DO YOU THINK?

- Why is it vital that you learn to read, write, and use math well?
- How can having short-term academic goals help you to make the most of your time in school?
- Why is it important for you to have some idea of the type of employment you would like after you leave school?

20

How can I get along with my teacher?

Name your favorite teacher. ....

Why do you like that teacher? ....

*Name the teacher you find it
hardest to get along with.* ....

YOU can choose your friends, but for much of your early life, you can't choose your teachers. Maybe you like all of them. David, 18, says: "I never really had problems with any of my teachers. I respected them, and they liked me."

On the other hand, you may have a teacher similar to the one described by 11-year-old Sarah. "She is super mean. And I can't understand her. She either doesn't explain enough about a lesson, or she describes way too much." To help you get along with your teacher, you first

"All things, therefore, that you want men to do to you, you also must likewise do to them."—Matthew 7:12.

• • • • • • • • •

need to identify the specific problem that you feel you have. Once you've pinpointed the challenge, you are better able to overcome it. Place a ✔ next to the appropriate box(es) below, or fill in your own reason.

❑ I find it difficult to understand my teacher
❑ I feel that I deserve higher grades
❑ I think that others receive preferential treatment
❑ I receive more discipline than I deserve
❑ I feel that I'm the victim of discrimination
❑ Other ....

What can help you to cope? A first step is to apply the counsel given by the apostle Peter. He wrote: "All of you be like-minded, showing fellow feeling." (1 Peter 3:8) What could possibly move you to have fellow feeling for a "mean" teacher? Consider some facts about teachers that might help you.

Teachers are fallible. They have their fair share of quirks, problems, and, yes, prejudices. "If anyone does not stumble in word," wrote the disciple James, "this one is a perfect man, able to bridle also his whole body." (James 3:2) Brianna, 19, says: "My math teacher wasn't very patient and would often scream at us. So we found it hard to respect her." What contributed to this situation? "The class was always chaotic," says Brianna, "and the kids would act crazy just to make the teacher more upset."

You no doubt appreciate it when a teacher overlooks your mistakes and shortcomings, especially if you've been under a lot of stress. Can you do the same for your teacher?

Write here about a recent incident at school and what you think might have provoked your teacher's behavior.

✎ ....

....

Teachers have favorites. Consider the challenges facing your teachers: How many of the students in your classes *want* to be there? How many of those who *do* want to be there are willing and able to concentrate on one topic for half an hour or more? How many students like to vent their pent-up frustrations and hostility on teachers? Now imagine that you had the job of teaching 20, 30, or even more of your peers and that the topic was one that few of them wanted to consider. Wouldn't you be inclined to give more attention to those who seemed interested?

True, it may irritate you when you see what seems to be blatant favoritism. Natasha says of one of her teachers: "He set a deadline for assignments but always made exceptions for the football players—and no one else. It just so happened that he was also the assistant coach of the team." If something similar happens to you, ask yourself, 'Are my educational needs being ignored?' If not, why be upset or jealous?

Write here what you could do to show your teacher more clearly that you are interested in what he or she is teaching.

....

....

....

Teachers misunderstand students. At times, a clash of

Teachers are like stepping-stones that can help you cross from ignorance to understanding, but you must do the walking

personalities or some sort of misunderstanding pits your teacher against you. Inquisitiveness may be viewed as rebellion, or a touch of wit, as disrespect or foolishness.

What can you do if you are misunderstood? The Bible says: "Return evil for evil to no one. . . . If possible, as far as it depends upon you, be peaceable with all men." (Romans 12:17, 18) So try not to antagonize your teacher. Avoid needless confrontations. Don't give your teacher legitimate causes for complaint. In fact, try to be friendly. 'Friendly? To *him?*' you ask. Yes, show manners by respectfully greeting your teacher when you come to class. Your persistent politeness—even a smile from time to time—just might change his opinion of you.—Romans 12:20, 21.

Ken, for example, had teachers who often misjudged him. "I'm very shy," he says, "and I would never talk to my teachers." How did he deal with the problem? "I eventually realized that for the most part, my teachers wanted to help me. So I made it a goal to get to know all my teachers personally. Once I did, I saw a huge improvement in my grades."

> **TIP**
>
> If you think your teacher is boring, focus on the topic, not the person. Take notes, respectfully ask for more information, and be enthusiastic about the subject. Enthusiasm is contagious.

> **I worked hard to be friends with all my teachers. I know their names, and if I see them on the street, I take a few minutes to chat with them.** —Carmen

True, friendly manners and talk will not always win over a teacher. But be patient. King Solomon wrote: "Patience and gentle talk can convince a ruler [or teacher] and overcome any problem." (Proverbs 25:15, *Contemporary English Version*) Remain calm and speak mildly when treated unfairly. Your teacher may reassess his opinion of you. —Proverbs 15:1.

If your teacher misunderstands you or treats you unfairly, what is usually your first reaction?

....

What would be a better reaction?

....

Resolving Specific Issues

Understanding your teacher's limitations is only a start. What can you do to resolve a specific issue? For example, how might you deal with the following complaints?

I deserve a better grade. "I always got A's," says Katrina. "But one year my science teacher gave me an F. I deserved better. My parents talked to the principal. But he only raised the grade to a D, so I was still pretty mad." If you face a similar issue, don't fire off a salvo of accusations against your teacher. Instead, learn from the Bible character Nathan. He had the difficult task of exposing a serious shortcoming on the part of King David. Nathan did not barge into the palace shouting accusations, but he approached David tactfully.—2 Samuel 12:1-7.

Likewise, you might humbly and *calmly* approach your teacher. If you throw a tantrum or accuse your teacher of incompetence or worse, you'll hardly win an ally. Try a more adult approach. Begin by asking your teacher to help you to understand his grading system. "Listen before you answer," wrote Solomon. "If you don't, you are being stupid and insulting." (Proverbs 18:13, *Today's English Version*) Once you've listened, you may be able to point out where you feel an oversight was made. Even if your grade is not changed, your maturity will probably make a positive impression on your teacher.

I feel that my teacher is prejudiced. Consider Rachel's experience. She had been receiving A's and B's on her report cards. Then, when she reached Grade 7, things changed. "My teacher did everything he could to make me fail his class," says Rachel. What was the problem? The teacher made it obvious to both Rachel and her mother that he did not like their religion.

action plan!

*To help me make a boring class more interesting,
I will*

....

....

*If I feel that my teacher is treating me unfairly,
I will*

....

....

*What I would like to ask my parent(s) about this
subject is*

....

....

What happened? Rachel says: "Each time it seemed clear that the teacher allowed his prejudice to affect the way he graded my work, Mom would come with me to discuss the matter with him. Eventually, he stopped giving me a hard time." If you experience a similar challenge, have the courage to speak to your parents about it. They, no doubt, will be interested in speaking to the teacher and possibly the school administration to work out a solution.

Take a Long-Range View

Admittedly, not all tangled affairs have neat endings. At times, you just have to endure. "One of my teachers had a bad attitude toward his students," says Tanya. "He often insulted us, calling us stupid. At first he made me cry, but I learned not to take his insults personally. I focused on my work and kept myself busy in his class. As a result, he didn't bother me much, and I was one of the few who received decent grades. After two years, that teacher was fired."

Learn how to cope with a difficult teacher, and you'll gain a valuable life skill—one that will serve you well when you have a difficult boss to deal with. You'll also learn to treasure good teachers when they come along.

IN OUR NEXT CHAPTER *Don't seem to have enough time in the day? Learn how to make the clock your friend, not your enemy.*

WHAT DO YOU THINK?

- Why is it important to focus more on the topic than on the teacher?

- How might your attitude toward a topic influence a teacher's attitude toward you?

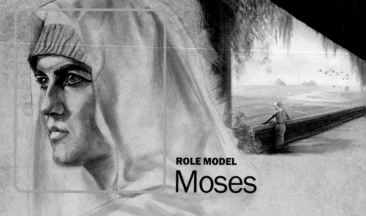

Moses

Moses has many **advantages** in life. He was raised in the royal household of Pharaoh and **educated** in all the **wisdom of Egypt.** (Acts 7:22) What will he do with his training? He could gain fame, fortune, and power. However, he is **not swayed** by peer pressure nor enticed by selfish ambition. Instead, he makes a career choice that no doubt **surprises many.** He chooses "to be ill-treated with the people of God." (Hebrews 11:25) Does Moses lose out? No. Because of choosing to **serve God** and **help people,** he enjoys an exciting, rewarding life.

If you are fortunate enough to have access to a good basic education, **what will you do** with that advantage? You could chase after money or power. Or, like Moses, you could do something **truly worthwhile** with your life. You could use your mental and physical assets to serve God and your neighbors. (Matthew 22:35-40) No other course of life is as rewarding!

21

How can I manage my time?

How many more hours could you use in a day?

✎ ....

What would you use the extra time for?

❏ To hang out with friends
❏ To sleep
❏ To study
❏ Other ....

TIME is like a spirited horse—if it is to work for you, you must learn to control it. Control your time, and you will likely reduce your stress, improve your grades, and gain more trust from your parents. "Sounds great," you say, "but it's easier said than done!" True, you will face challenges. But you can overcome them. Let's take some examples.

Challenge #1: Making a Schedule

What might stop you. Just the thought of *scheduling* makes you feel trapped! You like to be spontaneous, not tied to a plan.

Why do it anyway. King Solomon wrote: "The plans of the diligent one surely make for advantage." (Proverbs 21:5)

"Make sure of the more important things."
—Philippians 1:10.

. . . .

Solomon was a busy man. He was a husband, a father, and a king. And his life likely got busier as he grew older. Similarly, your life is busy now. But it will probably become more hectic as you grow older. Better that you become organized sooner rather than later!

What your peers say. *"About six months ago, I started planning my schedule regularly. I was trying to make things easier, and having a schedule seemed to do the trick!"* —Joey.

"Lists help keep me on track. When I have an extra-heavy load, my mom and I write it all down to figure out how we can help each other reach our goals."—Mallory.

What will help you. Look at it this way: Suppose you're going on a road trip. Each family member randomly throws his or her bags into the trunk of the car. It looks as though there won't be enough room for everything. What can you do? You might start again, putting the biggest bags in first and fitting the smaller bags into the remaining space.

The same strategy can be used to manage your life. If you start filling up your time with smaller things, you risk not being able to fit in the important things. Make space for the big things first, and you'll be amazed at how much more time you'll have for the rest!—Philippians 1:10.

What are the most important things you need to do?

✎ ....

....

....

Now go back and prioritize—number the things you need to do in order of importance. If you get the big things done first, you may be surprised at how much time you'll have left over to take care of the little things.

What you can do. Get a pocket planner, and prioritize what you need to do. On the other hand, perhaps one of the following alternatives below would work for you.

❑ Cell-phone calendar   ❑ Small notepad
❑ Computer calendar   ❑ Desk calendar

Challenge #2: Sticking to a Schedule

What might stop you. After school you just want to relax and watch TV for a *few minutes.* Or you plan to study for a test, but you get a text message inviting you to a movie. The movie won't wait, but you *can* put off studying until tonight. 'Besides,' you tell yourself, 'I seem to do better under pressure.'

Why do it anyway. You may earn a better grade if you study when your mind is more alert. Plus, don't you already have enough pressure to deal with? Why add to it by cramming for a test late at night? What will the next morning be like? You may oversleep, feel more stress, have to rush out the door, and possibly be late for school.—Proverbs 6: 10, 11.

What your peers say. *"I love watching TV, playing the guitar, and being with friends. These things aren't wrong; but sometimes they push the more important things back, and I end up rushing."—Julian.*

? **DID YOU KNOW . . .**

Scheduling too many activities into a day will cause you stress. If you set priorities, you will know which activities to pursue and which to drop.

What will help you. Don't just schedule things you have to do—schedule things you *enjoy.* "It's easier to do what I have to, knowing I have enjoyable things planned later," says Julian. Another idea: Have something to aim for, and then

Time is like a spirited horse
—you must learn to control it

set little goals along the way to make sure you're still on track.

What you can do. What are one or two realistic goals that you could achieve within the next six months?

✎..

....

What is a realistic goal you could achieve within the next two years, and what do you need to start doing now to reach that goal?*

....

....

Challenge #3: Being Neat and Organized

What might stop you. You're not sure how being neat and organized has anything to do with managing your time better. Besides, being messy seems so much easier. Cleaning your room can be done tomorrow—or not at all! You don't mind the mess, so it's really not a big deal. Or *is* it?

> **TIP** ✓
>
> **Don't try to apply all the suggestions made in this chapter at once. Instead, over the next month, apply just one of them. Once you've mastered that skill, choose another to work on.**

---

* For more information, see Chapter 39 of this book.

> *I overheard someone joking that if you wanted me to be somewhere by four o'clock, then you should tell me to be there by three. That's when I realized that I need to manage my time better!* —Ricky

Why do it anyway. Having everything neat and orderly will save you time when you are looking for your things. This will also give you much-needed peace of mind. —1 Corinthians 14:40.

What your peers say. *"Sometimes when I don't have time to put my clothes away, things I need find a way of getting lost under all the mess!"* —Mandy.

"I couldn't find my wallet for a week. I got pretty stressed over that. I finally found it when I cleaned my room." —Frank.

What will help you. Try to put things back in their place *as soon as you can.* Do it *regularly* rather than waiting until clutter gets out of control.

What you can do. Try making neatness a habit. Keep everything neater, and see if it makes life easier.

⟫⟫⟫ action plan!

The activity I can spend less time at is

✎ ....

I will use the time I gain to do the following

....

What I would like to ask my parent(s) about this subject is

....

....

:·where does my time go?

In a week's time, on average, youths between the ages of 8 and 18 spent their hours this way:

17 with their parents

30 at school

44 watching TV, playing video games, instant messaging, and listening to music

Add up the hours you spend each week

watching TV ✎ ....

playing video games ....

using the Internet ....

listening to music ....

Total ....

Hours I can easily
use for more
important things ....

Time is the one asset that you, your peers, and your parents all have the same amount of each day. Waste that asset, and you will suffer. Manage it wisely, and you will reap the rewards. The choice is up to you.

IN OUR NEXT CHAPTER *Are you the child of immigrant parents? Do you feel that you don't fit in either at school or at home? Learn how to turn your circumstances to your advantage.*

WHAT DO YOU THINK?

- How will learning to schedule your time now help you to manage your own home in the future?

- What lessons in time management can you learn from your parents?

- If you already use a schedule, what adjustments could you make for it to become more effective?

22

Caught between cultures—what can I do?

Is either your father or your mother an immigrant?

❏ Yes ❏ No

Is the language or culture that surrounds you at school different from that in your home?

❏ Yes ❏ No

"My family is Italian, and they openly express affection and warmth. We now live in Britain. Here people seem very orderly and polite. I feel out of place in both cultures—too Italian to be British and too British to be Italian."—Giosuè, England.

"At school my teacher told me to look at him when he spoke. But when I looked my Dad in the eye when he spoke, he said that I was being rude. I felt caught between two cultures."—Patrick, born in France to Algerian immigrant parents.

WHEN your parents migrated, they faced major challenges. Suddenly they were surrounded by people whose language, culture, and clothing were different from theirs. Now they stood out in a crowd. As a result, they may have been treated disrespectfully and may have become victims of prejudice.

Has that happened to you too? Listed below are some challenges that other youths in this situation have faced. Place a ✔ next to the one you find most difficult to deal with.

❏ **Ridicule.** Noor was a young girl when she and her family emigrated from Jordan to North America. "Our clothes were different, so people made fun of us," she says. "And we certainly didn't understand American humor."

❏ **An identity crisis.** "I was born in Germany," says a young girl named Nadia. "Since my parents are Italian, I spoke German with an accent, and the kids at school called me a 'stupid foreigner.' But when I visit Italy, I find that I speak Italian with a German accent. So I feel that I have no true identity. Wherever I go, I'm a foreigner."

❏ **A culture gap at home.** Ana was eight when she immigrated to England with her family. "For my brother and me, adapting to London was almost automatic," she says. "But it was challenging for my parents, who had lived for so long on the small Portuguese island of Madeira."

Voeun was three when she and her Cambodian parents arrived in Australia. "My parents have not adapted very well," she says. "In fact, Dad would often get upset and angry because I didn't understand his attitude and way of thinking."

❑ **A language barrier at home.** Ian was eight when he immigrated with his family to New York from Ecuador. After being in the United States for six years, he says: "Now I speak more English than Spanish. My teachers at school speak English, my friends speak English, and I speak English with my brother. English is filling my head and pushing the Spanish out."

DID YOU KNOW . . .

If you master two languages, you may boost your chances of finding employment.

Lee, who was born in Australia to Cambodian parents, says: "When I talk to my parents and want to elaborate on how I feel about certain matters, I find that I just can't speak their language well enough."

Noor, quoted earlier, says: "My father tried hard to insist that we speak his language at home, but we didn't want to speak Arabic. To us, learning Arabic seemed like extra baggage to carry. Our friends spoke English. The TV programs we watched were all in English. Why did we need Arabic?"

What Can You Do?

As the above comments show, you are not alone in facing these difficult challenges. Rather than deal with them,

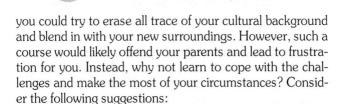

"God is not partial."—Acts 10:34.

• • • • • • • • •

you could try to erase all trace of your cultural background and blend in with your new surroundings. However, such a course would likely offend your parents and lead to frustration for you. Instead, why not learn to cope with the challenges and make the most of your circumstances? Consider the following suggestions:

How to view ridicule. No matter what you do, you are never going to be popular with everyone. People who enjoy ridiculing others will always find an excuse to do so. (Proverbs 18:24) So don't waste your breath trying to correct their prejudiced views. "Those who sneer at others don't like to be corrected," observed wise King Solomon. (Proverbs 15:12, *Contemporary English Version*) Prejudiced comments only expose the speaker's ignorance, not the victim's so-called faults.

How to deal with an identity crisis. It's only natural to want to belong to a group, such as a family or a culture. But it's a mistake to think that your worth is determined by your cultural or family background. People may judge you on that basis, but God doesn't. "God is not partial," said the apostle Peter. "In every nation the man that fears him and works righteousness is acceptable to him." (Acts 10:34, 35) If you do your best to please Jehovah God, he will view you as part of his family. (Isaiah 43:10; Mark 10:29, 30) What better identity could you have?

> **TIP** ✓
>
> If your peers make fun of your ethnic background, absorb their taunts while maintaining your sense of humor. If you do, they will likely lose interest in teasing you.

> *It makes me happy to be able to help others. I can explain the Bible to people who speak Russian, French, or Moldovan.* —Oleg

How to bridge the culture gap at home. Parents and children in almost every family will have differences in viewpoint. In your case, those differences might be amplified —your parents want you to live by the customs of the old country, but you want to adopt the customs of your new home. Even so, if you desire things to go well in your life, you must "honor your father and your mother."—Ephesians 6:2, 3.

Rather than rebelling against your parents' customs because they don't suit you, try to discern the reason why your parents respect those customs. (Proverbs 2:10, 11) Ask yourself the following questions: 'Do the customs conflict with Bible principles? If not, what specifically is it about the customs that I dislike? How could I respectfully convey my feelings to my parents?' (Acts 5:29) Of course, it will be much easier to honor your parents—to understand their thinking and express your feelings—if you know how to speak their language well.

How to overcome the language barrier at home. Some families have found that if they insist on speaking *only* their mother tongue while at home, the children will have the advantage of learning both languages well. Why not try that in your home? You may also want to ask your parents to help you learn to write the language. Stelios, who grew up in Germany but whose first language is Greek, says: "My parents used to discuss a Bible text with me each day. They would read it out loud, and then I would write it down. Now I can read and write both Greek and German."

You can choose to view your cultural background as a bridge that connects you with others

What's another payoff? "I learned my parents' language because I wanted to be close to them emotionally and, above all, spiritually," says Giosuè, quoted earlier. "Learning their language has allowed me to understand how they feel. And it has helped them to understand me."

A Bridge, Not a Barrier

Will you view your cultural background as a barrier that divides you from others or as a bridge that links you to them? Many young Christians have realized that they have an added reason for bridging the gap between cultures. They want to tell other immigrants about the good news of God's Kingdom. (Matthew 24:14; 28:19, 20) "Being able to explain the Scriptures in two languages is great!" says

⟫⟫⟫ action plan!

To improve my understanding of my parents' language, I will

✎ ....

....

What I would like to ask my parent(s) about this subject is

....

....

Salomão, who immigrated to London when he was five. "I had almost forgotten my first language, but now that I am in a Portuguese congregation, I can speak both English and Portuguese fluently."

Noor, quoted earlier, saw the need for evangelizers who could speak Arabic. She says: "Now I am taking classes and trying to pick up what I lost. My attitude has changed. Now I *want* to be corrected. I *want* to learn."

Certainly, if you are familiar with two cultures and can speak two or more languages, you have a real advantage. Your knowledge of two cultures increases your ability to understand people's feelings and to answer their questions about God. (Proverbs 15:23) "Because I understand two cultures," says Preeti, who was born in England to Indian parents, "I feel more comfortable in the ministry. I understand people from both ways of life—what they believe and what their attitudes are."

Can you too view your circumstances as an advantage rather than a liability? Remember, Jehovah loves you for who you are, not for where you or your family came from. Like the youths quoted here, can you use your knowledge and experience to help others of your ethnic background to learn about our impartial, loving God, Jehovah? Doing so can make you genuinely happy!—Acts 20:35.

WHAT DO YOU THINK?

- How can knowing about your parents' cultural background help you to understand yourself better?

- Compared with youths without a multicultural background, what advantages do you have?

Describe what sort of student you are and why you think you are that way.

✎

_____

_____

_____

_____

_____

_____

Write about some ways that school has benefited you.

_____

_____

_____

_____

_____

_____

_____

_____

_____

4 SEX, MORALS, AND LOVE

23

How can I explain the Bible's view of homosexuality?

The awards ceremony erupts into a frenzy when two popular actresses greet each other with a passionate kiss! Onlookers gasp in shock, then cheer in support. Gays call it a triumph. Skeptics call it a publicity stunt. Video clips of the kiss will be aired repeatedly on TV newscasts—and elicit millions of hits on the Internet—for days to come.

AS ILLUSTRATED in the above scenario, few events create more media buzz than when a celebrity hints at or comes out as being gay, lesbian, or bisexual. Some people praise such ones for their courage; others condemn them for their debauchery. Between the two viewpoints, many see homosexuality as nothing more than an alternative lifestyle. "When I was in school," says Daniel, 21, "even *straight* kids felt that if you had a problem with the idea of homosexuality, you were prejudiced and judgmental."

Attitudes about homosexuality may differ from one generation to another or from one land to another. But Christians aren't "carried hither and thither by every wind of teaching." (Ephesians 4:14) Instead, they adhere to the Bible's view.

What *is* the Bible's view of homosexuality? And if you live by the Bible's moral code, how can you respond to those who label you prejudiced, judgmental, or even homophobic? Consider the following questions or statements and possible responses.

"What does the Bible say about homosexuality?"

"The Bible makes it clear that God designed sex to be engaged in only between a male and a female and only within the arrangement of marriage. (Genesis 1:27, 28; Leviticus 18:22; Proverbs 5:18, 19) When the Bible condemns fornication, it is referring to both homosexual *and* illicit heterosexual conduct."*—Galatians 5:19-21.

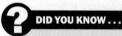

DID YOU KNOW . . .

Some first-century Christians who had engaged in homosexual acts in the past were able to change their unclean ways and be "washed clean" in God's sight.—1 Corinthians 6: 9-11.

"What's *your* view of homosexuality?"

"I don't hate homosexuals, but I can't approve of their conduct."

Remember: If you're guided by the Bible's moral code,

---

* The Bible term "fornication" refers not only to intercourse but also to such acts as masturbating another person or engaging in oral sex or anal sex.

READ MORE ABOUT THIS TOPIC IN VOLUME 2, CHAPTER 28

> **"Deaden, therefore, your body members that are upon the earth as respects fornication, uncleanness, sexual appetite, hurtful desire, and covetousness, which is idolatry."**—Colossians 3:5.

· · · · · · · · ·

then *that is your lifestyle choice, and you have a right to it.* (Joshua 24:15) Don't feel ashamed of your view.—Psalm 119:46.

"Shouldn't Christians respect all people, regardless of their sexual orientation?"

"Absolutely. The Bible says: 'Honor men of all sorts' or, as *Today's English Version* renders it, 'Respect everyone.' (1 Peter 2:17) Therefore, *Christians are not homophobic.* They show kindness to all people, including those who are gay."—Matthew 7:12.

"Doesn't your view of homosexuality encourage prejudice against gays?"

"Not at all. I reject homosexual *conduct,* not *people.*"

You could add: "To make a comparison, I also choose not to smoke. In fact, I find the very idea of it repugnant. But suppose you're a smoker and you feel differently. I wouldn't be prejudiced against you for your view, just as I'm sure you wouldn't be prejudiced against me for *my* view—am I right? The same principle applies to our differing views of homosexuality."

"Didn't Jesus preach tolerance? If so, shouldn't Christians take a permissive view of homosexuality?"

TIP
While the conduct of others might distress you, avoid a self-righteous tone. Really, they have the freedom to choose what they want to believe—just as you do.

∷ what about bisexuality?

Although found among both genders, bisexuality seems to be increasingly common among girls. For some, it's a matter of curiosity. Lisa, 26, says: "When you put something out there in movies, TV, and music that promotes girls kissing girls, teens will be tempted to try it —especially when they do not consider it to be wrong."

For others, there seems to be a genuine attraction. "I met two bisexual girls at a party," says Vicky, 13, "and later I found out from a friend that they liked me. Eventually I started texting one of the girls, and I started developing feelings for her."

Have you ever felt the way Vicky did? Many would urge you simply to embrace your sexuality and come out as bisexual. However, you should be aware that same-sex attraction *is often nothing more than a passing phase.* That's what Vicky found out. So did 16-year-old Lisette. She says: "Talking to my parents about my feelings made me feel better. Also, through my biology classes in school, I learned that during the adolescent years, hormone levels can fluctuate greatly. I truly think that if youths knew more about their bodies, they would understand that same-sex attraction can be temporary, and they wouldn't feel the pressure to be gay."

Even if your feelings seem more deep-rooted than a short-lived growing pain, realize that the Bible presents you with a reachable goal: You can choose not to act on wrong desires, no matter what they are.

"Jesus didn't encourage his followers to accept any and all lifestyles. Rather, he taught that the way to salvation is open to 'everyone *exercising faith in him.*' (John 3:16) Exercising faith in Jesus includes conforming to God's moral code, which forbids certain types of conduct—including homosexuality."—Romans 1:26, 27.

"Homosexuals can't change their orientation; they're born that way."

"The Bible doesn't comment on the biology of homosexuals, although it acknowledges that some traits are deeply ingrained. (2 Corinthians 10:4, 5) Even if some are oriented toward the same sex, the Bible tells Christians to shun homosexual acts."

Suggestion: Rather than get ensnared in a debate about the cause of homosexual *desires*, emphasize that the Bible prohibits homosexual *conduct*. To make a comparison, you could say: "You know, many claim that violent behavior can have a genetic root and that as a result, some people are predisposed to it. (Proverbs 29:22) What if that was true? As you might know, the Bible condemns fits of anger. (Psalm 37:8; Ephesians 4:31) Is that standard unfair just because some may be inclined toward violence?"

"How could God tell someone who is attracted to people of the same sex to shun homosexuality? That sounds cruel."

When it comes to popular opinion, Christians have the courage to walk against the crowd

> *A boy at school thought I was horrible for rejecting his lifestyle. But when I explained that I was not rejecting him as a person—and when he realized that it wasn't just homosexuality but all forms of immorality that I disagree with—he began to respect me and even defend me when others raised objections.* **—Aubrey**

"Such reasoning is based on the flawed notion that humans *must* act on their sexual impulses. The Bible dignifies humans by assuring them that they *can* choose not to act on their improper sexual urges if they truly want to."—Colossians 3:5.

"Even if you're not gay, you should change your view of homosexuality."

"Suppose I didn't approve of gambling but you did. Would it be reasonable for you to insist that I change

⟫⟫ action plan!

If someone says that the Bible's view of homosexuality is out-of-date, I will say

✎ ....

....

To make it clear that I disapprove of homosexual conduct, not the people themselves, I will say

....

....

What I would like to ask my parent(s) about this subject is

....

....

my view, simply because millions of people choose to gamble?"

Remember this: Homosexuals, along with most people, have some ethical code that causes them to deplore certain things—perhaps fraud, injustice, or war. The Bible prohibits those behaviors; it also draws the line at certain types of sexual conduct, including homosexuality.—1 Corinthians 6:9, 10.

The Bible is not unreasonable, nor does it promote prejudice. It simply directs those with homosexual urges to do the same thing that is required of those with an opposite-sex attraction—to "flee from fornication."—1 Corinthians 6:18.

The fact is, millions of *heterosexuals* who wish to conform to the Bible's standards employ self-control despite any temptations they might face. Their number includes many who are single with little prospect of marriage and many who are married to a disabled partner who is unable to function sexually. They are able to live happily without fulfilling their sexual urges. Those with homosexual inclinations can do the same if they truly want to please God. —Deuteronomy 30:19.

IN OUR NEXT CHAPTER *Some girls believe that having sex with their boyfriend will deepen their relationship with him. Not likely! Find out why.*

WHAT DO YOU THINK?

- **Why does God have the right to impose moral laws on humans?**

- **How do you benefit from adhering to the Bible's moral laws?**

24

Will sex improve our relationship?

Heather has been seeing Mike for only two months, but she feels as if she's known him forever. They text each other constantly, they talk for hours at a time on the phone, and they can even finish each other's sentences! But now, as they sit in a parked car under the moonlight, Mike wants more than conversation.

During the past two months, Mike and Heather have done nothing more than hold hands and briefly kiss. Heather doesn't want to go further. But she doesn't want to lose Mike either. No one makes her feel so beautiful, so special. 'Besides,' she tells herself, 'Mike and I are in love . . .'

YOU can probably guess where this scenario is heading. But what you may *not* realize is how dramatically sex would change things for Mike and Heather—and not for the better. Consider the following:

If you defy a physical law, such as the law of gravity, you suffer the consequences. The same is true if you defy a moral law, such as the one that states: "Abstain from fornication." (1 Thessalonians 4:3) What are the consequences of disobeying that command? The Bible says: "He that practices fornication is sinning against his own body." (1 Corinthians 6:18) How is that true? See if you can list below three harmful effects that can come to those who engage in premarital sex.

1 ....

2 ....

3 ....

Now look at what you wrote. Did you include such things as sexually transmitted disease, unwanted pregnancy, or the loss of God's favor? Those certainly are devastating consequences that can come to anyone who violates God's moral law regarding fornication.

Still, you might be tempted. 'Nothing will happen to *me*,' you could reason. After all, isn't *everyone* having sex? Your peers at school brag about their escapades, and *they* don't seem to be hurting. Perhaps, like Heather in the opening scenario, you even feel that sex will make you and your partner closer. Besides, who wants to be ridiculed for being a *virgin?* Isn't it better to give in?

Not so fast! First of all, not *everyone* is doing it. True, you may read statistics indicating that a large number of youths are having sex. For example, a U.S. study revealed that by the time they finish high school, 2 out of 3 youths in that country are sexually active. But that also means that 1 out of 3—a sizable number—are *not*. Now, what about those who *are?* Researchers have found that many such youths experience one or more of the following rude awakenings.

? DID YOU KNOW . . .

After having sex, a boy is more likely to abandon his girlfriend and move on to someone else.

RUDE AWAKENING 1 DISTRESS. Most youths who have engaged in premarital sex say that they regretted it afterward.

READ MORE ABOUT THIS TOPIC IN VOLUME 2, CHAPTERS 4 AND 5

> **"Flee from fornication. . . . He that practices fornication is sinning against his own body."**
> —1 Corinthians 6:18.

· · · · · · · · ·

RUDE AWAKENING 2 **DISTRUST.** After having sex, each partner begins to wonder, 'Who *else* has he/she had sex with?'

RUDE AWAKENING 3 **DISILLUSIONMENT.** Deep down, many girls would prefer someone who will *protect* them, not *use* them. And many boys find that they are less attracted to a girl who has given in to their advances.

In addition to the above, a number of boys have said that they would never marry a girl they have had sex with. Why? Because they prefer someone who is more chaste!

If you're a girl, does that surprise you—perhaps even anger you? Then remember this: The reality of premarital sex is far different from what is shown in movies and on TV. The entertainment industry glamorizes teen sex and makes it look like harmless fun or even true love. But don't be naive! Those who would try to coax you into premarital sex are only looking out for their own interests. (1 Corinthians 13:4, 5) After all, would anyone who *truly* loves you endanger your physical and emotional well-being? (Proverbs 5: 3, 4) And would anyone who *truly* cares for you tempt you to jeopardize your relationship with God?—Hebrews 13:4.

> **TIP** ✓
>
> **When it comes to conduct with the opposite sex, a good rule to follow is this: If it's something you wouldn't want your parents to observe you doing, then you shouldn't be doing it.**

> **As a Christian, you have qualities that will make you attractive to others. So you have to be alert and back off when invited to do something immoral. Respect those qualities. Don't sell out!** —Joshua

If you're a young man and you're dating, what has been stated in this chapter should give you reason to reflect on the relationship you're involved in. Ask yourself, 'Do I really care for my girlfriend?' If your answer is yes, how can you best show it? By having the *strength* to uphold God's laws, the *wisdom* to avoid tempting circumstances, and the *love* to look out for her interests. If you have such qualities, then likely your girlfriend's feelings will be similar to those of the morally upright Shulammite, who said: "My dear one is mine and I am his." (Song of Solomon 2:16) In short, you'll be her hero!

>>> action plan!

When I'm with a member of the opposite sex, the circumstances I need to avoid are

....

....

If a member of the opposite sex wants to meet me in a secluded place, I will say

....

....

What I would like to ask my parent(s) about this subject is

....

....

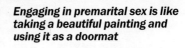

Engaging in premarital sex is like taking a beautiful painting and using it as a doormat

Whether you're a boy or a girl, if you were to give in to premarital sex, you would be degrading yourself by giving away something precious. (Romans 1:24) No wonder so many feel empty and worthless afterward, as if they've carelessly allowed a precious part of themselves to be stolen! Don't let that happen to you. If someone tries to coax you into sex by saying, "If you love me, you'll do this," firmly reply, "If you love *me*, you won't ask!"

Your body is far too valuable to give away. Show that you have the strength of character to obey God's command to abstain from fornication. Then, if you do marry one day, you *can* have sex. And you'll be able to enjoy it fully, without the worries, regrets, and insecurities that are so often the aftermath of premarital sex.—Proverbs 7:22, 23; 1 Corinthians 7:3.

IN OUR NEXT CHAPTER *How serious is the practice of masturbation?*

WHAT DO YOU THINK?

- Although premarital sex may appeal to the imperfect flesh, why is it wrong for you?

- What will you do if someone asks you to have sex?

25

How can I conquer the habit of masturbation?

"I began masturbating when I was eight years old. Later I learned God's view of the matter. I felt terrible every time I gave in. 'How could God love someone like me?' I asked myself."—Luiz.

WHEN you reach puberty, sexual desires can become particularly strong. As a result, you might fall into a habit of masturbation.* Many would say that it's not a big deal. "No one gets hurt," they argue. However, there's good reason to avoid the practice. The apostle Paul wrote: "Deaden, therefore, your body members . . . as respects . . . sexual appetite." (Colossians 3:5) Masturbation does not deaden sexual appetite but *fuels* it. In addition, consider the following:

● Masturbation instills attitudes that are totally self-centered. For example, when masturbating, a person is immersed in his or her own body sensations.

● Masturbation causes one to view those of the opposite sex as mere objects, or tools, for self-gratification.

● The selfish thinking that is instilled through the practice of masturbation can make satisfying sexual relations in marriage difficult to achieve.

Rather than resort to masturbation to relieve pent-up sexual urges, strive to cultivate self-control. (1 Thessalo-

---

* Masturbation is not to be confused with involuntary sexual arousal. For example, a boy might wake up sexually excited or have a nocturnal emission of semen. Similarly, some girls might find that they are stimulated unintentionally, particularly just before or after their menstrual period. In contrast, masturbation involves *deliberate* sexual self-stimulation.

nians 4:4, 5) To help you to do that, the Bible recommends that you avoid circumstances that might arouse you sexually in the first place. (Proverbs 5:8, 9) Still, what if you have become enslaved to the habit of masturbation? Perhaps you've tried to stop but without success. It would be easy to conclude that you're a lost cause, that you're incapable of living up to God's standards. That's how a boy named Pedro viewed himself. "When I relapsed, I felt terrible," he says. "I thought that I could never atone for what I had done. I found it hard to pray."

If that's how you feel, take courage. Your case isn't hopeless. Many young people—and adults—have overcome the habit of masturbation. You can too!

Dealing With Guilt

As already noted, those who have fallen into the habit of masturbation are often plagued with guilt. Without a doubt, being "saddened in a godly way" can give you the incentive to overcome the habit. (2 Corinthians 7:11) But excessive guilt can be counterproductive. It can make you feel so discouraged that you just want to give up the fight.—Proverbs 24:10.

So strive to put the matter in perspective. Masturbation is a form of uncleanness. It can make you a 'slave to various desires and pleasures,' and it fosters unhealthy attitudes. (Titus 3:3) At the same time, masturbation is not a form of gross sexual immorality, such as fornication. (Jude 7) If you have a problem with masturbation, you need not conclude

DID YOU KNOW . . .

Any weak person can give in to his or her sexual urges. But it takes a real man or a real woman to display self-control even when in private.

A fall while running does not mean that you have to start over—nor does a relapse with masturbation erase the progress you've already made

that you have committed the unforgivable sin. The key is to resist the urge and *never to give up your fight!*

It is easy to become downhearted after a relapse. When that occurs, take to heart the words of Proverbs 24:16: "The righteous one may fall even seven times, and he will certainly get up; but the wicked ones will be made to stumble by calamity." A temporary setback does not make you a wicked person. So do not give up. Instead, analyze what led to the relapse, and try to avoid repeating the same pattern.

Take time to meditate on God's love and mercy. The psalmist David, who was no stranger to personal weakness, stated: "As a father shows mercy to his sons, Jehovah has shown mercy to those fearing him. For he himself well knows the formation of us, remembering that we are dust." (Psalm 103:13, 14) Yes, Jehovah takes into consideration our imperfection and is "ready to forgive." (Psalm 86:5) On the other hand, he wants us to put forth effort to improve. So what practical steps can you take to conquer your habit?

Analyze your entertainment. Do you watch movies or TV programs or visit Web sites that are sexually stimulating?

TIP

Pray *before* urges become strong. Ask Jehovah God to give you "power beyond what is normal" to cope with temptation. —2 Corinthians 4:7.

"Flee from the desires incidental to youth, but pursue righteousness, faith, love, peace, along with those who call upon the Lord out of a clean heart."—2 Timothy 2:22.

• • • • • • • • •

The psalmist wisely prayed to God: "Make my eyes pass on from seeing what is worthless."*—Psalm 119:37.

Force your mind to focus on other matters. A Christian named William advises: "Before going to bed, read something related to spiritual things. It is very important that the last thought of the day be a spiritual one."—Philippians 4:8.

Talk to someone about the problem. Shame might make it difficult for you to bring up the matter to a confidant. Yet, doing so can help you to overcome the habit!

---

* For more information, see Volume 2, Chapter 33.

▶ action plan!

I can keep my mind on things that are chaste if I

....

....

Instead of giving in to the urge, I will

....

....

What I would like to ask my parent(s) about this subject is

....

....

> **Since overcoming the problem, I can keep a clean conscience before Jehovah, and that is something that I wouldn't trade for anything!** —Sarah

That's what a Christian named David found. "I talked privately with my father," he says. "I'll never forget what he said. With a reassuring smile on his face, he said, 'You make me so proud of you.' He knew what I had to go through to get to that point. No words could have lifted my spirits and determination more.

"My father then showed me a few scriptures to help me see that I was not 'too far gone,' and then some more scriptures to be sure I understood the seriousness of my wrong course. He said to 'keep the slate clean' until a certain time, and we would discuss it again then. He told me not to let it crush me if I relapsed, just go a longer period of time without giving in the next time." David's conclusion? He says: "Having someone else aware of my problem and helping me was the greatest benefit."*

---

* For more information, see Volume 2, pages 239-241.

IN OUR NEXT CHAPTER *Casual sex is no casual matter. Find out why.*

WHAT DO YOU THINK?

- Why is it important to remember that Jehovah is "ready to forgive"?—Psalm 86:5.

- Since God, who created sexual urges, also says that you should cultivate self-control, what confidence must he have in you?

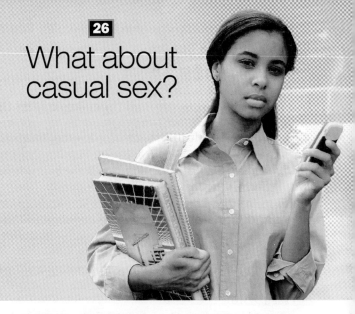

26

What about casual sex?

"Kids 'hook up' just to see how far they can go with each other and to see how many people they can have sex with."—Penny.

"Boys speak openly about it. They brag about how they have a girlfriend but still have sex with many other girls."—Edward.

MANY youths today boast of having casual sex with no emotional strings attached. Some even have acquaintances to whom they can turn for sex without the "complications" of a romance.

Don't be surprised if you feel tempted by that prospect! (Jeremiah 17:9) Edward, quoted earlier, says: "Many girls have offered me sex, and resisting is the most difficult struggle I have as a Christian. It's hard to say no!" What

Bible principles should you keep in mind if you are invited to have casual sex?

Know Why Casual Sex Is Wrong

Fornication is so serious a sin that those who practice it "will not inherit God's kingdom." (1 Corinthians 6:9, 10) Of course, that's true whether two people are "in love" or engaging in casual sex. To resist temptation in either situation, you must view the practice of fornication as Jehovah does.

"I firmly believe that Jehovah's way is the best way to live."—Karen, Canada.

"Remember that you are somebody's son or daughter, a friend to many people, and part of a congregation. You would let all these people down if you gave in!"—Peter, Britain.

By adopting Jehovah's view of fornication, you will be able to "hate what is bad," even if it appeals to the flesh. —Psalm 97:10.

Suggested reading: Genesis 39:7-9. Notice Joseph's brave stand against sexual temptation and what enabled him to resist.

? DID YOU KNOW . . .

Jehovah wants you to enjoy sex as he created it to be—a source of pleasure within marriage—without the worries, insecurities, and regrets that are so often by-products of fornication.

Be Proud of Your Beliefs

It's not unusual for youths to stand up proudly for a cause they believe in. Your privilege is to uphold God's standards by your conduct. Don't be ashamed of your view of premarital sex.

"Make it clear right from the start that you have moral principles."—Allen, Germany.

> **Be strong! When a young man made a sug-gestive invitation to me, I said, 'Get your hand off my shoulder!' and I walked away with a stern look.** —*Ellen*

"*The boys I went to high school with knew who I was, and they knew that their attempts would be a waste of their breath.*"—*Vicky, United States.*

Taking a stand for your beliefs is a sign that you are becoming a mature Christian.—1 Corinthians 14:20.

Suggested reading: Proverbs 27:11. See how your positive actions can move Jehovah's heart!

Be Decisive!

Saying no is important. But some might misread your refusal as playing "hard to get."

"*Everything about you—including how you dress, how you talk, who you talk to, and how you relate to people—should convey your refusal.*"—*Joy, Nigeria.*

"*You need to make it clear that it is never going to happen. Never accept gifts from boys who are trying to get their way with you. They can use it against you, as if you owe them something in return.*"—*Lara, Britain.*

Jehovah will help you if you show yourself to be decisive. Based on his personal experience, the psalmist David could say of Jehovah: "With someone loyal you will act in loyalty."—Psalm 18:25.

TIP

Work on your inner qualities. (1 Peter 3: 3, 4) The better you are as a person, the better kind of person you'll attract.

> **"Do your utmost to be found finally by [God] spotless and unblemished and in peace."**
> —2 Peter 3:14.

. . . .

Suggested reading: 2 Chronicles 16:9. Note that Jehovah is eager to help those who want to do what is right.

Use Foresight

The Bible states: "Shrewd is the one that has seen the calamity and proceeds to conceal himself." (Proverbs 22:3) How can you apply that to yourself? By using foresight!

"Separate yourself as much as possible from people who talk about such things."—Naomi, Japan.

"Don't give out personal information, such as your address or phone number."—Diana, Britain.

Analyze your speech, conduct, and associations, as well as the places you frequent. Then ask yourself, 'Am I unwit-

>>> **action plan!**

I can imitate Joseph's resolve to remain morally clean if I

✎ ....

....

I will avoid the mistake Dinah made if I

....

....

What I would like to ask my parent(s) about this subject is

....

....

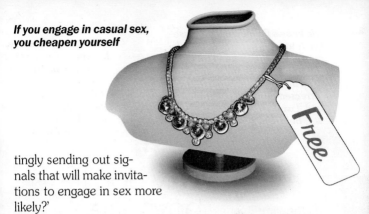

If you engage in casual sex, you cheapen yourself

tingly sending out signals that will make invitations to engage in sex more likely?'

Suggested reading: Genesis 34:1, 2. See how being in the wrong place had tragic consequences for a girl named Dinah.

Remember, casual sex is no casual matter to Jehovah God; neither should it be to you. By taking a stand for what's right, you can preserve a clean conscience before God and maintain self-respect. As a girl named Carly puts it, "why let yourself be 'used' for someone else's instant gratification? Take care of what you have worked so hard to maintain!"

IN OUR NEXT CHAPTER *What kind of girls do boys say they're really attracted to? You might be surprised!*

WHAT DO YOU THINK?

- Although illicit sex may appeal to the imperfect flesh, why is it wrong?
- What will you do if someone asks you to have sex?

DO YOU worry that boys are not attracted to you? Many girls do, even the ones you think would have no problems! Take Joanne, for example. She's good-looking, intelligent, and articulate. Yet, she says: "I often feel that boys don't like me. A few that I liked showed an interest in me for a while but later stopped talking to me completely!"

What types of things do young men find attractive in a girl? What do they find *unattractive*? What can you do to catch the attention of a decent young man?

What to Do

● **Know your own mind and heart.** You likely felt an increased attraction to boys soon after you entered puberty. You may have felt drawn to more than one boy. That's normal. But if you had quickly given your heart to the first boy who made your pulse race, you would have risked stunting your emotional and spiritual growth. It takes time to develop positive personality traits, to 'make your mind over' on important matters, and to reach some of your *own* goals.—Romans 12:2; 1 Corinthians 7:36; Colossians 3:9, 10.

True, many boys are attracted to girls who have not yet formed strong convictions or who are naive. However, such boys are primarily interested in the girl's body, not in who she is as a person. The fact is, a balanced young man will look for a girl who can bring her strengths to a partnership.—Matthew 19:6.

What boys say: "I find it attractive when a girl is able to form opinions for herself, when she seems to have the inner conviction that she's a person in her own right."—James.

> **I admit that I'm often initially attracted to pretty girls. But that can quickly cool off if the girl doesn't have some definite, worthwhile goals. On the other hand, if she knows what she wants to do with her life—especially if she has already reached some of her goals—that can make her very attractive.** —Damien

"I'd be interested in a girl who can express herself in an honest, respectful way and who doesn't just agree with everything I say. Even if she's pretty, I don't feel comfortable with a girl who just says what I want to hear."—Darren.

What is your reaction to the boys' comments above?

✎ ....

....

● **Develop respect for others.** Just as you have a need for love, the boys you know have a deep desire for respect. It's no coincidence that the Bible says to the husband that he should love his wife but that the wife should have "deep respect" for her husband. (Ephesians 5:33) In harmony with this insight, one survey of hundreds of young men found that more than 60 percent said that they valued respect *more* than love. Over 70 percent of the older men surveyed made that same choice.

Respect doesn't mean surrender—that you must give up your right to hold a different opinion and to express it. (Genesis 21:10-12) But the *way* you express your opinion will likely determine if you attract or repel a young man. If you consistently contradict or correct what he says, he may feel that you have little respect for him. Yet, if you acknowledge his viewpoint and comment on what you find praiseworthy, he will be more likely to accept and value your opin-

Love and respect are like the two wheels of a bicycle —both are essential

ion. Of course, a discerning young man will also notice if you treat members of your family and others with respect.

What boys say: *"I think respect is the most important thing at the start of a relationship. Love might develop later."—Adrian.*

"If a girl can show respect for me, I feel that she can definitely love me."—Mark.

What is your reaction to the boys' comments above?

....

....

● **Dress modestly, and maintain good hygiene.** Your dress and grooming are like loudspeakers that broadcast your inner thoughts and attitudes. Long before you start to talk to a boy, your attire has expressed volumes about you. If your clothing is well-arranged and modest, it will send a very positive message. (1 Timothy 2:9) If it is provocative or sloppy, the message will be loud and clear —and negative!

> **TIP** ✔
>
> Go easy on the makeup! Too much can send the wrong message—that you are conceited or even desperate for attention.

What boys say: *"A girl's standard of dress says a lot about her attitude toward life. If she wears revealing or sloppy clothes, it tells me that she is desperate for attention."*—Adrian.

"I am drawn to a girl who cares for her hair, smells pleasant, and has a soothing tone of voice. On the other hand, although I was attracted to one beautiful girl, her bad hygiene put an end to that."—Ryan.

"If a girl dresses provocatively, she'll spark an initial attraction for sure. But that's not the type of girl I want to start a relationship with."—Nicholas.

What is your reaction to the boys' comments above?

✎ ....

....

What Not to Do

● **Don't flirt.** Women have the ability to exert tremendous influence on men. That power to attract can be used for good and for bad. (Genesis 29:17, 18; Proverbs 7:6-23) If you test out the power you have on every boy you meet, you'll likely gain a reputation as a flirt.

What boys say: *"Just sitting beside an attractive girl and touching shoulders can be thrilling, so I think that a girl who frequently touches you when talking to you is flirting."*—Nicholas.

"If a girl constantly finds ways to touch the arm of every boy she meets or if she coyly glances at every passing male, then I think she's a flirt, and I find that unattractive."—José.

● **Don't be clingy.** When a couple marry, they become what the Bible calls "one flesh." (Genesis 2:24) At that stage of the relationship, both husband and wife give up many of the freedoms they may have had when single; really, they become committed to each other. (1 Corinthians 7:32-34) However, if you're just getting to know a young man, you don't have the right to expect that level of accountability from him, nor he from you.* The fact is, when you recognize his right to enjoy other friends, he may become more intrigued by you. And the way he uses that freedom will tell you much about his character.—Proverbs 20:11.

What boys say: "*I think a girl is being too clingy if she needs to know my every move and seems incapable of having a social life or other interests aside from me.*"—Darren.

"*If a girl I've recently met constantly texts me and wants to know who is with me, especially the names of any girls in the group, then I think that's a warning sign.*"—Ryan.

"*A girl who won't allow you to spend time with your male friends and gets annoyed when you don't always invite her to be with you is unattractively dependent.*"—Adrian.

---

* Of course, when a couple get engaged, they are rightly more accountable to each other.

⟫⟫⟫ action plan!

The trait that I will give attention to improving is

✎ ....

....

What I would like to ask my parent(s) about this subject is

....

....

> "Charm may be false, and prettiness may be vain; but the woman that fears Jehovah is the one that procures praise for herself."
> —Proverbs 31:30.

• • • • • • • •

What is your reaction to the boys' comments in this sub-heading?

✎ ....

....

Appreciate Your Own Value

You likely know girls who would do anything just to gain the attention and approval of a boy. Others may lower their standards just so they can have a boyfriend—or even a husband. However, the principle 'you reap what you sow' applies in this matter. (Galatians 6:7-9) If you don't value yourself and the standards you try to live by, you're likely to attract boys who don't value you or your standards either.

The fact is, not all boys will like you—and that can be a good thing! But if you are conscious of caring for both your outer beauty and your inner beauty, you will have "great value in the eyes of God"—and you will attract the type of young man that will suit you best.—1 Peter 3:4.

IN OUR NEXT CHAPTER *What if you're a boy and you've wondered, 'Why don't girls like me?'*

WHAT DO YOU THINK?

- How can you show that you respect a young man's thoughts and feelings?
- How can you show that you value yourself?

YOU'RE old enough to date. You'd like to find someone who is attractive and who shares your religious beliefs. (1 Corinthians 7:39) In the past, though, each time you tried to start a relationship, you felt as though you crashed and burned. What went wrong? Are girls looking only for the best-looking boys? "Some muscles on him can't hurt," admits a girl named Lisa. Still, most girls are looking for something more. "The good-looking boys don't always have substance," says 18-year-old Carrie.

What's involved in having "substance"? If you'd like to get to know a girl better, what factors do you need to consider? And what Bible principles would you do well to remember?

What to Do First

Before you decide to pursue your interest in a particular girl, there are some basic skills you need to master, and these will help you to be friends with *anyone*. Consider the following.

● **Cultivate good manners.** The Bible says that "love is not ill-mannered." (1 Corinthians 13:5, *Today's English Version*) Good manners show that you respect others and that you're developing a mature, Christlike personality. However, good manners aren't like a suit you wear to impress others but take off when you get home. Ask yourself, 'Do I display good manners when dealing with my family members?' If not, then it will seem forced when you do so while interacting with others outside your home. Remember, to find out the type of person you really are, a dis-

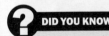

DID YOU KNOW...

How you look on the outside is less important than what you are on the inside.

"Put on the new personality which was created according to God's will in true righteousness and loyalty."—Ephesians 4:24.

• • • • • • • •

cerning girl will look at the way you treat members of your family.—Ephesians 6:1, 2.

What girls say: *"I definitely find it attractive if a boy displays good manners both in small things, like opening the door for me, and larger things, like being kind and considerate not only to me but also to my family."*—Tina.

"I am put off when I've just met someone but he asks questions that are too personal, such as 'Are you dating?' and 'What are your goals?' It's rude and makes me squirm!"—Kathy.

"I find it disrespectful when boys think they can play with our emotions, as if our feelings don't matter and we are all so desperate to get married that we want them to take pity on us."—Alexis.

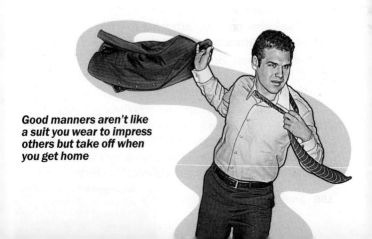

Good manners aren't like a suit you wear to impress others but take off when you get home

> **Boys think that to attract girls they have to dress a certain way or have a certain look. While this is true to some degree, I think that many girls are more attracted to positive personality traits.** —Kate

● **Maintain your personal hygiene.** Good hygiene shows respect not only for others but also for yourself. (Matthew 7:12) If you respect yourself, others are more likely to respect you. On the other hand, if you let your hygiene slide, you'll sabotage your efforts to impress a girl.

What girls say: "One boy who was interested in me had really bad breath. I just couldn't get past that."—Kelly.

● **Cultivate conversation skills.** The basis of a lasting relationship is good communication. You discuss not only *your* interests but also the interests of *your* friend. (Philippians 2:3, 4) You really listen to what she has to say and you value her opinions.

What girls say: "I'm impressed when a boy can converse with me naturally—when he can remember things I told him and can ask questions that keep the conversation moving."—Christine.

"I think that boys are attracted to what they see, but girls are more attracted to what they hear."—Laura.

"Gifts are great. But if a boy can hold a good conversation, if he can comfort and encourage you with his words . . . Wow! That's attractive."—Amy.

"I know one young man who is polite and never overly familiar. We can actually have meaningful conversations without his saying things like, 'You smell really good' or 'You look very cute today.' He really listens to what I say, and that would make any girl feel good."—Beth.

READ MORE ABOUT THIS TOPIC
IN VOLUME 2, CHAPTER 3

"I would definitely want to get to know someone better if he had a sense of humor but could also talk about more serious things without sounding fake."—Kelly.

● **Be responsible.** The Bible says: "We each must carry our own load." (Galatians 6:5, *Contemporary English Version*) Girls won't be attracted to a young man who can't hold down a job because he is lazy or because he spends too much time at play.

What girls say: "I wish some boys would take on more responsibility. It's a definite turn-off when they don't. It doesn't give a good impression."—Carrie.

"Some boys don't have their goals straight. If they're interested in a girl, they find out what her goals are and they say, 'Wow, that's what I want to do!' But their present actions prove the opposite."—Beth.

Being responsible, as illustrated above, will help you to enjoy good friendships. However, once you feel that you are ready to start a serious relationship with a particular girl, what should you do?

The Next Step

● **Take the initiative.** If you think a friend whom you admire might make a good marriage mate, let her know you are interested in her. Be clear and forthright in declaring your feelings. Yes, it can be nerve-racking. You fear rejection. But your being willing to take the initiative is a sign that you have grown up. One caution, though: This isn't a marriage proposal. So be discerning. An overly somber or

> **TIP**
>
> Ask a few mature adults what skill they think is most important for a young man to develop, and determine whether this is an area you need to work on.

overly earnest approach may intimidate a girl rather than attract her.

What girls say: *"I can't read minds. So if someone wanted to get to know me better, he would have to be honest and straightforward and just tell me."*—Nina.

"It could be an awkward transition if you've been friends for a while. But I'd respect someone if he simply said that he would like to get to know me as more than just a friend."—Helen.

● **Respect the girl's decision.** What if your friend says that she doesn't want a more serious relationship with you? Dignify her by believing that she knows her own heart and that her no means no. It betrays a lack of maturity if you make a pest of yourself. Really, if you ignore a girl's explicit rejection of your attention—even becoming provoked by her rebuff—are you really thinking of her interests or your own?—1 Corinthians 13:11.

What girls say: *"It irritates me when I say a definite no to a boy but he keeps on trying."*—Colleen.

"I explained to one boy that I wasn't interested in him, but he kept pressuring me for my phone number. I wanted to be nice. After all, it probably wasn't easy for him to work up the nerve to express his feelings. But eventually I had to be very firm with him."—Sarah.

What Not to Do

Some young men feel that they have little trouble getting girls to like them. They may even compete with their peers to show who can grab the attention of the most girls. However, such competition is cruel and will earn you a bad reputation. (Proverbs 20:11) You can avoid that outcome if you keep the following in mind.

● **Don't flirt.** A flirt uses flattering speech and provocative body language. He has no intention of pursuing an honorable romantic relationship. Such actions and attitudes ignore the Bible's counsel to treat "younger women as sisters with all chasteness." (1 Timothy 5:2) Flirts make poor friends and worse marriage mates. Discerning girls know that.

What girls say: *"I think it's very unattractive when someone flatters you but you know that he has said the same things to your friend just last month."—Helen.*

"This cute boy once started flirting with me, talking mainly about himself. When another girl joined our group, he did the same with her. Then a third girl joined our group, and he used the same lines on her. It was ugly!" —Tina.

● **Don't toy with a girl's feelings.** Don't expect that friendship with a member of the opposite sex will operate

action plan!

One area in which I could become more mannerly is

✎ ....

....

To improve my conversation skills,
I will

....

....

What I would like to ask my parent(s) about this subject is

....

....

according to the same rules as friendship with a member of the same sex. Why? Consider: If you remarked that a male friend looked good in his new suit or you regularly talked to that friend and confided in him, it is unlikely that he would think that you are romantically attracted to him. But if you compliment a girl on her appearance or you regularly talk to her and confide in her, she may well think that you have a romantic interest in her.

What girls say: *"I just don't think boys understand that they can't treat girls the same way that they treat their male friends."—Sheryl.*

"A boy will get my phone number, and then I get a text message from him. So, . . . what does that mean? Sometimes you can have a text-messaging relationship and get emotionally attached, but how much can you say in a text message?"—Mallory.

"I don't think a boy realizes how quickly a girl can become emotionally involved, especially if he is caring and easy to talk to. It's not that she's desperate. I just think that most girls want to fall in love and that they always have an eye out for 'Mr. Right.'"—Alison.

IN OUR NEXT CHAPTER *How can you tell the difference between love and infatuation?*

WHAT DO YOU THINK?

- How can you show that you respect yourself?
- How can you show that you respect a girl's thoughts and feelings?

29

How do I know if it's real love?

Answer the following questions:

1. How would you define "love"?

....

....

2. How would you define "infatuation"?

....

....

3. What, in your opinion, is the difference between the two?

....

....

YOU likely had little or no trouble answering the questions above. After all, it's easy to see the difference between love and infatuation when you're just thinking hypothetically.

All of that can change, though, the moment you set your eyes on the boy or girl of your dreams. Suddenly you're smitten, and nothing else matters. You're hopelessly in love. Or *are* you? Is it love—or is it infatuation? How can you tell? To answer, first let's consider how your view of the opposite sex has probably changed in recent years. For example, consider the following questions:

● What did you think of the opposite sex when you were five years old?

● What do you think of the opposite sex *now?*

Your answers likely reveal that when you hit puberty, you gained a new appreciation for the opposite sex. "I've noticed that girls are a little prettier than they used to be," says 12-year-old Brian. Elaine, 16, recalls a change that took place a few years ago. "All my girlfriends started talking about boys," she says, "and for me, every boy was a potential crush."

Now that you're noticing the opposite sex, how can you cope with these powerful feelings? Instead of pretending that they don't exist—a surefire way to intensify them—you can use this as a wonderful opportunity to learn something about attraction, infatuation, and love. Understanding these three facets of romance can spare you needless heartache and help you, in time, to find real love.

ATTRACTION ➡ What you see

"My friends and I are always talking about girls. We try to discuss other things, but as soon as a pretty girl walks by, well, we forget what we were talking about!"—Alex.

"A young man who makes eye contact and has a nice smile and a confident walk would get my attention." —Laurie.

DID YOU KNOW . . .

Young people who frivolously enter and exit romantic relationships are, in a sense, "practicing" for divorce after marriage.

It's normal to be attracted to someone who is outwardly beautiful or handsome. The problem is, what you see isn't always what you get. Why? Be-

READ MORE ABOUT THIS TOPIC IN VOLUME 2, CHAPTERS 1 AND 3

"Many waters themselves are not able to extinguish love, nor can rivers themselves wash it away."—Song of Solomon 8:7.

• • • • • • • •

cause looks can be deceiving. The Bible states: "As a gold nose ring in the snout of a pig, so is a woman that is pretty but that is turning away from sensibleness." (Proverbs 11: 22) Of course, the same principle applies to boys.

INFATUATION ➡ What you feel

"I had a major crush on a boy when I was 12, and when I got over it, I realized why I liked him. It was only because all my friends were interested in boys—and he was a boy. So there you go!"—Elaine.

"I've had many crushes, but most of the time, I was only considering the outer person. Once I found out what the person was like on the inside, I realized that we weren't as compatible as I had thought."—Mark.

Infatuation *feels* like love. In fact, love *includes* romantic feelings. But the basis for each is entirely different. Infatuation stems from a superficial reaction to surface qualities. Also, it is blind to the other person's weaknesses and exaggerates his or her strengths. As a result, infatuation is about as stable as a castle made of sand. "It doesn't last long," says a girl named Fiona. "You can be attracted to someone one day, and then a month later you feel the same way—but toward someone else!"

> **TIP** ✓
>
> To find out how well you really know someone you feel attracted to, answer the questions on the worksheet in Volume 2, on page 39 (for girls) and page 40 (for boys).

Infatuation is about as stable as a castle made of sand—in a short time, it washes away

LOVE ➡ What you know

"I think that with love, you have a reason to be attracted to someone, and it's a good reason—not a selfish one." —David.

"To me, it seems that real love should grow over time. At first, you're good friends. Then, little by little, you like what you have come to know about the person, and you start to develop feelings that you've never had before."—Judith.

Love is based on a well-rounded knowledge of a person's strengths and weaknesses. It's hardly surprising, then, that the Bible describes love as much more than a feeling. It states that love is, among other things, "long-suffering and kind. . . . It bears all things, believes all things, hopes all things, endures all things. Love never fails." (1 Corinthians 13:4, 7, 8) And love makes a person act in these ways based on knowledge—not on credulity or ignorance.

An Example of Real Love

The Bible account of Jacob and Rachel vividly illustrates real love. The couple met at a well, where Rachel had gone to water her father's sheep. Jacob was immediately attracted to her. Why? For one thing, she was "shapely and beautiful."—Genesis 29:17, *Today's English Version*.

Remember, though, that real love is based on more than physical appearance. Jacob found that there was more to Rachel than her beauty. In fact, the Bible says that before long, Jacob was beyond the stage of attraction. He was "in love with Rachel."—Genesis 29:18.

Romantic ending? No—because the story was far from over. Rachel's father made Jacob wait *seven years* before he could marry Rachel. Fair or unfair, Jacob's love was now put to the test. If it were a case of mere infatuation, Jacob would not have waited for her. Only real love can endure the test of time. So what happened? The Bible states: "Jacob proceeded to serve seven years for Rachel, but in his eyes they proved to be like some few days because of his love for her."—Genesis 29:20.

What can you learn from the example of Jacob and Rachel? That real love can pass the test of time. Also, it's not

⟫⟫ action plan!

To help me determine whether my feelings for someone are an indication of infatuation or of love, I will

....

....

What I would like to ask my parent(s) about this subject is

....

....

based solely on physical appearance. In fact, a potential marriage mate may not be someone you find overwhelmingly attractive at first sight. Barbara, for example, met a young man to whom she admits she was not overly attracted—at first. "But as I got to know him better," she recalls, "things changed. I saw Stephen's concern for other people and how he always put the interests of others before himself. These were the qualities I knew would make a good husband. I was drawn to him and began to love him." A solid marriage resulted.

When you're mature enough to date with a view to marriage, how will you know when you've found real love? Your heart may speak, but trust your Bible-trained mind. Get to know more than the person's external image. Give the relationship time to blossom. Remember, infatuation often fades within a short time. Genuine love grows stronger with time and becomes "a perfect bond of union."—Colossians 3:14.

Be assured that you can find that kind of love—*if* you learn to look beyond attraction (what you see) and infatuation (what you feel). The following three pages will help you to do just that.

IN OUR NEXT CHAPTER *Suppose you've found true love. How do you know if you're ready for marriage?*

WHAT DO YOU THINK?

- Why did God create humans with such powerful feelings of attraction to the opposite sex?

- Why do many teenage "love" relationships fail?

∴ what would *you* do?

Michael and Judy have been seeing each other for three months, and Judy says she's "hopelessly in love." Michael dotes on her constantly—even telling her how to dress and with whom she can and cannot associate. He treated her like a princess—until last week. Michael slapped Judy after she was "caught" talking to another boy.

He says: *"Judy should know that I'm terrified of losing her. In fact, the thought of another guy stealing my girlfriend just drives me crazy! I feel bad about slapping Judy. But that's how much I can't bear to see her even look at someone else. Besides, I apologized!"*

She says: *"My parents say Mike is controlling, but he just has high standards. I mean, he's never tried to force me to do anything sexually. And when he slapped me—which I didn't tell my parents about—well, I was talking to another boy. And Mike gets jealous, which I sometimes find flattering. Anyway, he said he's sorry, and he promised he'd never do it again."*

Your turn: Do you see warning signs in this relationship? If so, what are they?

✎ ....

....

What should Judy do?

....

....

What would you do?

....

....

◌ what would *you* do?

Ethan has been dating Alyssa for two months, and he's already noticed how contentious Alyssa can be, especially with her parents. In fact, Alyssa argues with her parents constantly, and she usually wins. She's mastered the "art" of holding her position until her parents back down in exhaustion. Alyssa has bragged to Ethan that she has her parents "wrapped around her finger."

He says: *"Alyssa speaks her mind. She doesn't take anything from anyone—including her parents. Her dad can be annoying, and it's no wonder that she loses her temper with him. But it's not all yelling. Alyssa can cry, pout, or act all sweet—whatever it takes to get what she wants from Dad and Mom."*

She says: *"I don't care who you are or what title or position you hold, I'll talk straight to you, and I may not sugarcoat my words. My boyfriend, Ethan, knows that about me. He's seen me around my parents."*

Your turn: Do you see warning signs in this relationship? If so, what are they?

....

....

What should Ethan do?

....

....

....

What would you do?

....

....

....

∷ is it love or is it infatuation?

Try to guess the missing word in the statements quoted below. Fill in the blanks with either the word **love** or the word **infatuation**.

1. "............................ is blind and it likes to stay that way. It doesn't like to look at reality."—Calvin.

2. "If I have to change my personality when I'm around a girl I'm attracted to, that's ...."—Thomas.

3. "Something may annoy you about the person. But if it's ...., you still want to be with the person and work through the problem."—Ryan.

4. "With ...., the only things you let yourself consider are the things you have in common."—Claudia.

5. "When it's ...., you don't try to hide who you are."—Eve.

6. "............................ is a selfish form of getting what you want—perhaps just to say you have a boyfriend."—Allison.

7. "............................ recognizes the faults and quirks and yet can still live with those things."—April.

8. "When it's ...., you can't define why you feel attracted—you just are."—David.

9. "With ...., the other person can do no wrong."—Chelsea.

10. "When it's ...., you don't notice other members of the opposite sex the way you used to, because you feel a sense of loyalty."—Daniel.

Answers: Infatuation: 1, 2, 4, 6, 8, 9. Love: 3, 5, 7, 10.

30

You've found your match, and you've been dating long enough to know that you're in love. Wedded bliss is on the horizon. Or is it? On the threshold of one of life's biggest decisions, you start to wonder . . .

Are we *really* ready for marriage?

NAGGING doubts about marriage are normal—even when you're in love. With unhappy marriages abounding and divorce rates soaring, it's under-

standable that you want to proceed with caution as you contemplate this life-altering step. How do you know if you're ready for it? Now more than ever, you need to root out any daydreams you may have about marriage and replace them with realities. For example:

DAYDREAM 1 **"We can live on love."**

Reality: Love will neither pay bills nor cover over financial hardship. In fact, researchers have found money to be a leading cause of marital disputes and eventual divorce. An unbalanced view of money can cause you spiritual and emotional harm, and it can erode your relationship with your spouse. (1 Timothy 6:9, 10) The lesson? Don't wait until *after* marriage to discuss money management!

The Bible says: "Who of you that wants to build a tower does not first sit down and calculate the expense?"—Luke 14:28.

Suggestion: Talk over your future financial arrangements with your intended spouse now—*before* you are married. (Proverbs 13:10) Consider such questions as these: How will our income be budgeted? Will we have a joint bank account or separate accounts? Which spouse will be more adept at keeping financial records and seeing that bills are paid?* How much money can one of us spend on a purchase without consulting the other? *Now* is the time to start working as a team!—Ecclesiastes 4:9, 10.

DAYDREAM 2 **"We'll be a perfect match as a married couple because we see eye to eye on everything—we never disagree!"**

Reality: If you never disagree, it's probably because you've carefully managed to avoid issues that might spark a

---

* The "capable wife" of Proverbs 31:10-28 is portrayed as handling a number of weighty responsibilities that had a direct bearing on family finances. See verses 13, 14, 16, 18, and 24.

"A man will leave his father and his mother and he must stick to his wife and they must become one flesh."—Genesis 2:24.

• • • • • • • • •

conflict. But marriage will not afford you that luxury! The fact is, *no* two imperfect humans are perfectly matched, so a measure of disagreement is inevitable. (Romans 3:23; James 3:2) You need to consider not only how well you agree but also what happens when you disagree. A strong union is made up of two people who can openly acknowledge a difference and then work to settle the matter maturely and amicably.

The Bible says: "Don't go to bed angry."—Ephesians 4:26, *Contemporary English Version.*

Suggestion: Reflect carefully on how you've handled conflict with your parents and siblings up to this point. Make a chart similar to the one that appears on page 93 of this book or on page 221 of Volume 2. Note specific events that have triggered a disagreement, how you responded, and what response might have been better. For example, if your impulsive reaction to a conflict has been to storm off to your room and angrily slam the door, write down a better response—one that will work to resolve the problem rather er than further entrench it. If you learn to respond better to conflict now, you'll gain a skill that is crucial to a happy marriage.

TIP

Talk to an older married couple, and ask them what advice they would give to a new husband and wife about how to have a successful marriage.—Proverbs 27:17.

DAYDREAM 3 "Once I get married, all my sexual desires will be satisfied."

Reality: Being married does *not* guarantee 'sex on

(Continued on page 218)

Ruth

The widow Ruth knows about **loyalty.** She has chosen to stay by the side of her aged mother-in-law, Naomi, rather than return to a more comfortable life in her hometown. Even though this choice lessens her chances of finding a mate, Ruth **keeps focused** on the big picture. Her **love for Naomi** and her **desire to be with Jehovah's people** mean more to her than impulsively satisfying her desire for marriage.—Ruth 1:8-17.

Are you thinking about marriage? Then imitate Ruth. Look beyond your emotions, and ask what positive qualities you would bring to a future mate. For example, are you **loyal** and **self-sacrificing?** Do you **conform to Godly principles,** even when your imperfect flesh begs you to do otherwise? Ruth did not desperately seek a mate. However, in time, she found a husband who proved to be a **mature man** who shared similar qualities—above all, a **love for God.** The same outcome could be true for you.

⋗ are you ready to get married?

Consider the questions on the following two pages. You might even use these pages as a basis for discussion between you and your future mate. Be sure to look up the cited scriptures.

financial issues

☐ *What is your attitude toward money?*—Hebrews 13:5, 6.

☐ *In what ways do you already show yourself to be financially responsible?*—Matthew 6:19-21.

☐ *Are you currently in debt? If so, what steps are you taking to pay off what you owe?*—Proverbs 22:7.

☐ *What will be the cost of your wedding? How much debt, if any, would you consider reasonable?*—Luke 14:28.

☐ *After you are married, will both you and your spouse need to work? If so, how will you handle differing schedules and transportation needs?*—Proverbs 15:22.

☐ *Where will you and your spouse live? How much will rent, food, clothing, and other expenses likely cost, and how will you pay for those expenses?*—Proverbs 24:27.

family matters

☐ *How well do you get along with your parents and siblings?*—Exodus 20:12; Romans 12:18.

☐ *How do you currently resolve conflicts at home?*
—Colossians 3:13.

☐ *If you are a young woman, in what ways do you demonstrate a "quiet and mild spirit"?*—1 Peter 3:4.

☐ *Do you plan to have children?* (Psalm 127:3) *If not, what form of birth control will you use?*

☐ *If you are a young man, how do you plan to take the lead in providing spiritually for your family?*—Matthew 5:3.

personality traits

☐ *In what ways have you shown yourself to be industrious?*—Proverbs 6:9-11; 31:17, 19, 21, 22, 27.

☐ *How have you demonstrated a self-sacrificing spirit?*
—Philippians 2:4.

☐ *If you are a young man, in what ways do you show that you can handle authority in a Christlike manner?*
—Ephesians 5:25, 28, 29.

☐ *If you are a young woman, what evidence is there that you can subject yourself to authority?*—Ephesians 5:22-24.

(*Continued from page 214*)

demand.' Remember, your spouse is a human being who has feelings that *must* be considered. Frankly, there will be times when your mate simply isn't in the mood for intimacy. Marriage does not give you the right to insist on having your needs fulfilled. (1 Corinthians 10:24) The fact is, self-control is vital in both singleness *and* marriage.—Galatians 5:22, 23.

The Bible says: "Each one of you should know how to get possession of his own vessel in sanctification and honor, not in covetous sexual appetite."—1 Thessalonians 4: 4, 5.

Suggestion: Make a careful review of your sexual desires and tendencies, and think about how these might affect your future marriage. For example, are you enslaved to the self-focused habit of masturbation? Have you had a habit of viewing pornography? Do you have a roving eye, secretly looking lustfully at members of the opposite sex? Ask yourself, 'If I have trouble controlling my sexual desires *before* marriage, how will I be able to do so afterward?' (Matthew 5:27, 28) Another matter: Have you been prone to flirt and play the field, earning a reputation as a playboy or a flirt among those of the opposite sex? If so, how do you plan to curtail that tendency after marriage, when your affections will need to be directed to one person—your spouse?—Proverbs 5:15-17.

DID YOU KNOW ...

In a successful marriage, husband and wife view each other as friends, communicate well, know how to resolve conflicts, and view their relationship as a lifelong union.

DAYDREAM 4 "Marriage will make me happy."

Reality: An unhappy single person usually becomes an unhappy married person. Why? Because happiness is

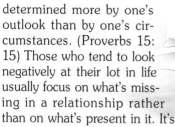

Do not jump into marriage without first knowing something about the "waters" you are getting into

determined more by one's outlook than by one's circumstances. (Proverbs 15: 15) Those who tend to look negatively at their lot in life usually focus on what's missing in a relationship rather than on what's present in it. It's far better to cultivate and nurture a positive spirit while single. Then, when you're married, you'll bring out the best in yourself and your spouse.

The Bible says: "It is better to be satisfied with what you have than to be always wanting something else."—Ecclesiastes 6:9, *Today's English Version.*

Suggestion: Sometimes a negative attitude comes from having unrealistic expectations. On a separate sheet of paper, list two or three expectations you have of marriage. Read them, and then ask yourself: 'Are my expectations

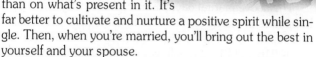

⟫⟫ action plan!

The trait I will work on now to help improve my relationship with my future spouse is

✎ ....

What I would like to ask my parent(s) about this subject is

....

....

> *Marriage is a huge step. It's important to know not only what you're getting into but who you're getting into it with.* —Audra

based more on fantasy than on reality? Have they been fueled by the media, perhaps by romantic movies or books? Do my expectations focus on what marriage will do for *me* —perhaps cure *my* chronic loneliness, satisfy *my* desire for sex, upgrade *my* status among my peers?' If so, you will need to shift from thinking about "me" to thinking about "us." To help you do that, list two or three expectations of marriage that involve you *and* your future spouse.

The above marital daydreams can adversely affect your happiness in marriage. So strive to eliminate such thinking and replace it with a realistic outlook. The worksheet on pages 216 and 217 can help you and your future spouse as you look forward to what can be one of life's greatest blessings—a happy marriage!—Deuteronomy 24:5; Proverbs 5:18.

IN OUR NEXT CHAPTER *A breakup can feel like a minideath. How can you cope with the aftermath?*

WHAT DO YOU THINK?

- In some lands, a high percentage of marriages end in divorce. Why, do you think, is that the case?

- What dangers are there in marrying simply to escape an unhappy homelife?

- Why will it be important to conform to Bible principles in your future marriage?

31

How can I get over a breakup?

"We'd been dating for six months and had been friends for five years. When he wanted to end the relationship, he couldn't even face me. He just stopped talking to me. I felt helpless. The disappointment was overwhelming. I kept asking myself, 'What did I do wrong?'"—Rachel.

A BREAKUP can crush your joyful disposition and replace it with tearful despair. Consider Jeff and Susan, who dated for two years. Over that period their emotional bond grew. Throughout the day, Jeff sent Susan text messages with expressions of endearment. From time to time, he gave her gifts to show that he was thinking of her. "Jeff put forth an effort to listen to me and understand me," Susan says. "He made me feel special."

Before long, Jeff and Susan were talking about marriage and where they would live as husband and wife. Jeff even inquired about Susan's ring size. Then, quite suddenly, he called off the relationship! Susan was devastated. She went through the motions of daily life, but she felt numb with shock. "I became mentally and physically exhausted," she says.*

Why It Hurts

If you've been in a situation similar to that of Susan, you might well wonder, *'Will I ever be able to move on?'* Your distress is understandable. "Love is as powerful as death," wrote King Solomon. (Song of Solomon 8:6, *Today's English Version*) So, breaking up may be one of the most traumatic experiences you've ever had to endure. In fact, some have said that a breakup is like a minideath. You may even find yourself going through these and perhaps other typical stages of grief:

Denial. *'It can't be over. He'll change his mind in a day or two.'*

Anger. *'How could he do this to me? I can't stand him!'*

DID YOU KNOW . . .

The vast majority of teen-dating relationships do not lead to marriage, and those that do have a high rate of divorce.

---

* Although the individuals quoted in this chapter are female, the principles discussed apply to males as well.

Depression. *'I'm unlovable. No one will ever love me.'*

Acceptance. *'I'm going to be all right. The breakup hurt, but I'm getting better.'*

The good news is that you *can* reach the acceptance stage. How much time it will take to get there depends on a number of factors, including how long your relationship lasted and how far it progressed. In the meantime, how can you cope with your heartbreak?

TIP ✔

Susan, mentioned at the outset of this chapter, made a list of scriptures and kept it handy so that she could read those texts when she felt overwhelmed by her emotions. Perhaps you can do the same with some of the scriptures cited in this chapter.

Moving Forward

You may have heard the saying, Time heals all wounds. When you first break up, those words might ring hollow. That's because time is only part of the solution. To illustrate: A cut on your skin will heal *in time,* but it hurts *now.* You need to stop the bleeding and soothe the pain. You also need to keep it from becoming infected. The same is true with an emotional wound. Right now, it hurts. But there are steps you can take to lessen the pain and keep from becoming

A breakup is like a painful cut—it hurts, but in time it will heal

:: what can I learn from the breakup?

Were you given a reason for the breakup? If so, write the reason below, regardless of whether you feel it was valid.

✎...

....

What other reasons, do you think, might have been involved?

....

....

....

In hindsight, is there anything you could have done that would have changed the outcome? If so, what?

....

....

....

Has this experience revealed any areas in which you would like to grow spiritually or emotionally?

....

....

....

What, if anything, would you do differently in your next relationship?

....

....

....

....

"[Jehovah] is healing the brokenhearted ones, and is binding up their painful spots."
—Psalm 147:3.

• • • • • • • •

infected with bitterness. Time will do its part, but how can you do yours? Try the following.

● **Allow yourself to grieve.** There's nothing wrong with having a good cry. After all, the Bible says that there is "a time to weep" and even "a time to wail." (Ecclesiastes 3:1, 4) Shedding tears doesn't mean you're weak. In the midst of emotional anguish, even David—a courageous warrior—once admitted: "Every night my bed is damp from my weeping; my pillow is soaked with tears."—Psalm 6:6, *Today's English Version*.

● **Take care of your physical health.** Physical exercise and proper nutrition will help replenish the energy lost as a result of the emotional toll of a breakup. "Bodily training is beneficial," the Bible says.—1 Timothy 4:8.

What areas pertaining to your health might you need to give attention to?

....

....

....

● **Keep busy.** Don't stop doing the things that interest you. And now, more than ever, don't isolate yourself. (Proverbs 18:1) Associating with those who care about you will give you something positive on which to focus.

What goals can you set?

....

....

....

● **Pray to God about your feelings.** This might be a challenge. After a breakup, some even feel betrayed by God. They reason, 'I prayed and prayed that I would *find* someone, and *now* look at what happened!' (Psalm 10:1) Would it be right, though, to view God as merely a celestial matchmaker? Surely not; nor is he responsible when one party does not wish the relationship to continue. We do know this about Jehovah: *"He cares for you."* (1 Peter 5:7) So pour out your feelings to him in prayer. The Bible states: "Let your petitions be made known to God; and the peace of God that excels all thought will guard your hearts and your mental powers by means of Christ Jesus."—Philippians 4:6, 7.

What specific things could you pray to Jehovah about while you are striving to cope with the anguish of a breakup?

....
....
....

>>> action plan!

To help me to move on after a breakup,
I will

....
....

What I could work on to be a better partner in my next dating relationship is

....
....

What I would like to ask my parent(s) about this subject is

....
....

> *Time gives you a much clearer perspective. Later, your emotions won't be running so high, so you can think about the situation objectively and get some closure. Also, you can find out more about who you are and what you would look for in a mate, as well as what to guard against to avoid a similar situation in the future.* —Corrina

Looking Ahead

After you've had time to heal, you might do well to take a close look at just what happened in your past relationship. When you're ready to do that, you may find it helpful to write out your responses to the questions in the box "What Can I Learn From the Breakup?" on page 224.

Granted, the relationship you were involved in didn't become what you had hoped. But remember this: In the middle of a storm, it's easy to focus on the dark sky and the pouring rain. Eventually, though, the rain stops and the sky clears. The youths quoted earlier in this chapter found that they were, in time, able to move on. Be assured that the same can be true of you!

IN OUR NEXT CHAPTER *What steps can you take to protect yourself from sexual predators?*

WHAT DO YOU THINK?

● What have you learned about yourself from your past relationship?

● What have you learned about the opposite sex?

Each year, millions of people are raped or otherwise sexually abused, and research shows that young people are a prime target. For example, it's estimated that in the United States, about half of all rape victims are under 18 years of age. Because of the prevalence of abuse, it is vital that you consider this topic.

32

How can I protect myself from sexual predators?

"He grabbed me and threw me down before I knew what was happening. I tried everything I could to fight him off. I pulled out a can of pepper spray, but he knocked it away. I tried to scream, but only air escaped my lungs. I pushed, kicked, punched, and scratched. And that's when I felt a knife pierce my skin. I went completely limp."—Annette.

SEXUAL predators run rampant today, and young people are often the target of their attack. Some youths, like Annette, are assaulted by a stranger. Others are attacked by a neighbor. Such was the case with Natalie, who at just 10 years of age was sexually abused by a teenager who lived near her home. "I was so scared and ashamed that at first I didn't tell anyone," she says.

Many youths have been molested by a family member. "Between the ages of 5 and 12, I was sexually abused by my father," says a woman named Carmen. "I finally confronted him about it when I was 20. He said he was sorry, but a few months later, he kicked me out of the house."

Sexual abuse at the hands of a neighbor, friend, or family member is disturbingly common today.* But the exploitation of young people is nothing new. Such deplorable conduct took place even in the days when the Bible was written. (Joel 3:3; Matthew 2:16) Today we live in critical times. Many people lack "natural affection," and it's common for girls (and even boys) to be taken advantage of sexually. (2 Timothy 3:1-3) While no precaution *guarantees* your safety, there is much you can do to protect yourself. Consider the following tips:

Be alert. As you walk outdoors, know what is happening ahead of you, behind you, and on both sides. Some areas are known to be dangerous, especially at night. To the extent possible, either avoid those areas or at least make sure you're not alone.—Proverbs 27:12.

Don't send mixed messages. Avoid flirting or dressing provocatively. Such actions may send the message that you're interested in getting physical—or at least that you wouldn't object to it.—1 Timothy 2:9, 10.

Talk about boundaries. If you're dating, discuss with the other person what conduct is and is not appropriate.# Once you have set boundaries, do not put yourself in compromising situations in which you could be abused.—Proverbs 13:10.

Be willing to speak up. There's nothing wrong with firmly stating, "Don't do that!" or "Take your hand off me!" Don't hold back out of fear that you'll lose your boyfriend. If

---

* Some cases involve date rape, in which a girl is either forced to have sex or is drugged into compliance.

For more information, see Volume 2, Chapter 4.

☙ "if you love me . . . "

One type of sexual predator doesn't force himself on girls but cleverly plays on their emotions. How? By saying such things as, "Everyone else has sex," "No one will ever find out," or, as mentioned in Chapter 24 of this book, "If you love me, you'll do this." Don't be conned by a boy who tries to make you believe that sex equals love. The fact is, anyone who thinks that way is only looking out for his own gratification. He is *not* thinking of you or your welfare. In contrast, a real man will put your interests above his own and will show that he has the strength to uphold God's moral standards. (1 Corinthians 10:24) A real man won't treat girls as sex objects. Instead, he will view "younger women as sisters with all chasteness."—1 Timothy 5:1, 2.

he breaks up with you over this issue, he's not worth keeping! After all, you deserve a real man, one who respects your body and your principles.*

Be cautious while online. Never give out personal information or post photos that identify your whereabouts.#
If you receive a sexually explicit message, usually the best reply is *no* reply. A wall of silence renders most online predators powerless.

The preceding steps can make you less vulnerable to

? **DID YOU KNOW . . .**

In the United States, more than 90 percent of juvenile victims of sexual assault know their attacker.

* Of course, that advice also applies if a girl pressures a boy for sex.

\# For more information, see Volume 2, Chapter 11.

> **"In the last days critical times hard to deal with will be here. For men will be lovers of themselves, . . . having no natural affection, . . . without self-control, fierce, without love of goodness."**—2 Timothy 3:1-3.

• • • • • • • • •

attack. (Proverbs 22:3) Realistically, though, you may not always be in full control of your circumstances. For instance, you might not always be able to have a traveling companion or to avoid dangerous areas. You may even *live* in a dangerous area.

Perhaps you know through bitter experience that bad things can happen despite your efforts to avoid trouble. Like Annette, quoted at the outset, you may have been caught unawares and been overpowered. Or like Carmen, you may have been victimized as a child and, as such, were powerless to control the situation—or even to understand fully what was happening. How can you deal with the guilt that often torments those who have been sexually abused?

Coping With Guilt

Annette still struggles with guilt over what occurred. "I'm my own worst enemy," she says. "I keep playing that night over and over again in my head. I feel as though I should have tried harder to fight him off. The fact is, after being stabbed, I was paralyzed with fear. I couldn't do anything more, but I feel that I *should* have."

TIP ✔
If you have been the victim of sexual abuse, keep a list of scriptures that can comfort you. These might include Psalm 37:28; 46:1; 118: 5-9; Proverbs 17:17; and Philippians 4:6, 7.

> **It's very hard to speak up about the abuse, but it's the best thing you can do. Speaking up helps you to let go of your sadness and anger and to regain your power.** —Natalie

Natalie also struggles with guilt. "I shouldn't have been so trusting," she says. "My parents had a rule that my sister and I had to stay together when we played outside, but I didn't listen. So I feel I gave my neighbor the opportunity to hurt me. What happened affected my family, and I feel responsible for causing them so much pain. I struggle with that the most."

If your feelings are similar to those of Annette or Natalie, how can you cope with guilt? First, try to keep foremost in mind that if you were raped, *you were not a willing participant.* Some people trivialize the issue, using the excuse that "boys will be boys" and that victims of rape were asking for it. But no one deserves to be raped. If you were the victim of such a heinous act, *you are not to blame!*

Of course, reading the statement "you are not to blame" is easy; believing it may be much more difficult. Some keep what happened bottled up inside and are racked with guilt and other negative emotions. However, who is best served by silence—you or the abuser? You owe it to yourself to consider another option.

Telling Your Story

The Bible tells us that in the height of his personal turmoil, the righteous man Job said: "I will give vent to my concern about myself. I will speak in the bitterness of my soul!" (Job 10:1) You will benefit from doing the same. Talking to a trusted confidant about what happened can in time help you to come to terms with the rape and gain relief from your distressing emotions.

In fact, if you are a Christian, it is important that you speak to a congregation elder about what happened. The comforting words of a loving shepherd can assure you that as a victim of rape, you have not been defiled by someone else's sin. That's what Annette found. She says: "I talked to a close friend, and she urged me to speak with a couple of Christian elders in my congregation. I'm glad I did. They sat down with me on several occasions and told me exactly what I needed to hear—that what happened was not my fault. *None* of it was my fault."

The feelings left by abuse might be too heavy for you to carry by yourself. Why not get help by talking to someone?

⟫⟫⟫ action plan!

When I feel guilty about what happened, I will

✎ ....

....

What I would like to ask my parent(s) about this subject is

....

....

Talking about what happened and expressing your feelings can keep you from becoming consumed with anger and resentment. (Psalm 37:8) It may also help you to gain relief, perhaps for the first time in years. After she told her parents about the abuse, Natalie found that to be true. "They supported me," she says. "They encouraged me to talk about it, and that helped me not to be so sad and angry inside." Natalie also found comfort in prayer. "Talking to God helped me," she says, "especially at those times when I felt that I couldn't open up to another human. When I pray, I can speak freely. It gives me a real sense of peace and calm."*

You too can find that there is "a time to heal." (Ecclesiastes 3:3) Rely on supportive friends who are like the elders described as being similar to "a hiding place from the wind and a place of concealment from the rainstorm." (Isaiah 32:2) Take care of yourself physically and emotionally. Get needed rest. And most of all, rely on the God of all comfort, Jehovah, who will soon bring about a new world in which "evildoers themselves will be cut off, but those hoping in Jehovah are the ones that will possess the earth."—Psalm 37:9.

---

* Sometimes victims of abuse are subject to severe depression. In such a case, it might be wise to consult a physician. For more information on coping with distressing feelings, see Chapters 13 and 14 of this book.

WHAT DO YOU THINK?

- **What are the benefits of speaking up about abuse?**

- **What could happen—to you and to others—if you keep silent?**

Write out three personal policies that you are determined to live by. Include why you believe that each policy is wise.*

✎ 1. _____

_____

_____

_____

_____

2. _____

_____

_____

_____

3. _____

_____

_____

_____

_____

* For example, "I will refrain from sex until I am married, and I believe that this is the best course because . . ." Make sure that what you write expresses *your* moral convictions, not simply those of someone else.

5 SELF-DESTRUCTIVE BEHAVIOR

33

What should I know about smoking?

Look at the following options, and put a ✔ in the box beside each item that you feel describes you.

- ❏ I'm curious
- ❏ I'm dealing with stress
- ❏ I want to fit in
- ❏ I'm concerned about my weight

IF YOU checked *any* of the boxes on page 237, then you have something in common with your peers who smoke tobacco or have thought about it.* For example:

Satisfying curiosity. "I wondered what it was like, so I took a cigarette from a girl at school and then sneaked out and smoked it."—Tracy.

Coping with stress and fitting in. "Kids at school would say 'I *need* a cigarette,' and then afterward, 'Phew, now I can cope!' During stressful times, I wanted that."—Nikki.

Losing weight. "Some girls smoke to stay thin—it's so much easier than dieting!"—Samantha.

But before you light your first—or your next—cigarette, stop and think. Don't be like a fish striking at a baited hook. True, the fish may get a small reward, but what a price it pays! Instead, follow the Bible's advice, and use "your clear thinking faculties." (2 Peter 3:1) Answer the following questions.

What Do You Really Know About Smoking?

Mark each statement true or false.

a. Smoking will reduce my stress. ❏ True ❏ False

b. I would exhale almost all of the smoke. ❏ True ❏ False

c. Smoking won't affect my health until I get older. ❏ True ❏ False

d. Smoking will make me more attractive to the opposite sex. ❏ True ❏ False

e. If I smoke, no one is hurt but me. ❏ True ❏ False

f. It doesn't matter to God whether I smoke or not. ❏ True ❏ False

---

* Although this chapter discusses those who smoke cigarettes, the problems and dangers that are highlighted also apply to those who chew tobacco.

Like a fish striking at bait, a smoker gets a reward but pays a terrible price

Answers

a. *False.* Although smoking temporarily relieves the stress of withdrawal symptoms, scientists have found that nicotine actually increases the level of stress hormones.

b. *False.* Some studies indicate that over 80 percent of the cigarette smoke particles you inhale stay inside your body.

c. *False.* While the risks increase with each cigarette you smoke, a few effects are immediate. Some people become addicted from just one cigarette. Your lung capacity will be reduced, and you'll likely develop a persistent cough. Your skin will wrinkle more and prematurely. Smoking increases your risk of sexual dysfunction, panic attacks, and depression.

d. *False.* Researcher Lloyd Johnston found that teens who smoke are "less attractive to the great majority of the opposite sex."

e. *False.* Secondhand smoke kills thousands each year; it will harm your family, your friends, and even your pets.

f. *False.* Those who want to please God must cleanse

> **DID YOU KNOW...** ❓
>
> **Smokeless tobacco —such as chewing tobacco—can deliver more nicotine than cigarettes and contains some 25 cancer-causing toxins that increase the user's risk of developing cancer of the throat and mouth.**

> **When I'm offered a smoke, I just smile and say, 'No thanks, I don't want to get cancer.'**
> *—Alana*

themselves of "every defilement of flesh." (2 Corinthians 7:1) There is no doubt that smoking defiles the body. If you choose to be unclean, harming yourself and others by using tobacco, you cannot be a friend of God.—Matthew 22:39; Galatians 5:19-21.

How to Resist

So, what will you do if someone offers you a cigarette? A simple but firm response, such as "No thanks, I don't smoke," will often work. If the person persists or even taunts you, remember that it is your choice. You might say:

● "I checked out the risks and decided that it's not for me."

● "I have some important future plans that involve breathing."

● "Are you denying my right to make a personal choice?"

Like the youths quoted earlier in this chapter, though, you may find that the greatest pressure comes from inside yourself. If that's the case, answer this 'inner voice' by reasoning on questions such as these:

● 'Will I really gain benefits from smoking? For instance, if I decide to smoke just to be accepted by others, will I somehow fit in despite having little else in common with them? Do I even *want* to fit in with people who would be happy to see me damage my own health?'

● 'How much will smoking cost me in money, health problems, and loss of others' respect?'

● 'Would I be willing to sell out my friendship with God for the price of a cigarette?'

⁝ is marijuana really that bad?

"Some say that using marijuana is a way to escape problems," says Ellen, who lives in Ireland, "and that it doesn't have any bad side effects." Have you heard similar statements about marijuana? Compare some common myths with the facts.

Myth. Marijuana is not harmful.

Fact. Known or suspected lasting effects of marijuana are as follows: damaged memory, impaired ability to learn, and suppressed immune system, as well as damage to the sexual health of both males and females. It can induce anxiety attacks, psychoses, and paranoia. Children born to women who smoke marijuana are more likely to have behavioral problems, be less attentive, and have greater difficulty making decisions.

Myth. Marijuana smoke is less harmful than cigarette smoke.

Fact. Compared with tobacco smoke, marijuana smoke can deposit four times as much tar on your airways and carry five times as much poisonous carbon monoxide into your blood. Smoking five marijuana joints can deliver the same amount of cancer-causing toxins as an entire pack of cigarettes.

Myth. Marijuana is not addictive.

Fact. Teens who have mental or emotional problems can quickly become addicted to marijuana. Others can become addicted after long-term use. In addition, studies show that teens who smoke marijuana have a much greater risk of using other addictive drugs, such as cocaine.

TIP

Avoid rationalizations, such as thinking, 'I'll only take one puff.' They often lead to a full relapse.—Jeremiah 17:9.

What, though, if you're already hooked? What can you do to break free?

How to Quit

1. Be Convinced. Write down *your* reasons for quitting, and review this list regularly. A desire to be clean before God can be a powerful motive.—Romans 12:1; Ephesians 4: 17-19.

2. Get help. If you've been smoking in secret, now is the time to come clean. Tell those you have been hiding your smoking from that you are quitting, and ask for their support. If you want to serve God, pray for his help.—1 John 5:14.

3. Set a quit date. Give yourself two weeks or less, and mark on your calendar the day you are determined to quit. Tell your family and friends that you are quitting on that date.

4. Search and destroy. Before you reach your quit date, scour your room, car, and clothing for any cigarettes. Destroy them. Get rid of lighters, matches, and ashtrays.

⟫⟫ action plan!

If a schoolmate pressures me to smoke, I will

✎ ....

....

What I would like to ask my parent(s) about this subject is

....

....

> **"Stay away from everything that keeps our bodies . . . from being clean."**
> —2 Corinthians 7:1, *Contemporary English Version.*

• • • • • • • • •

5. Deal with withdrawal symptoms. Drink plenty of fruit juice or water, and allow yourself more time for sleep. Keep in mind that the discomfort is *temporary*, while the benefits are *permanent!*

6. Avoid triggers. Stay away from situations and places where you would be tempted to smoke. You may also need to cut off social contact with associates who are smokers. —Proverbs 13:20.

Don't Be Duped

Each year, tobacco companies spend billions of dollars on advertising. Whom do they particularly target? An internal tobacco company document states: "Today's teenager is tomorrow's potential regular customer."

Don't allow tobacco executives to get their hands into your pockets. Why take their bait? Neither that group nor your peers who smoke have your best interests at heart. Rather than listen to them, listen to the advice found in the Bible and learn "to benefit yourself."—Isaiah 48:17.

IN OUR NEXT CHAPTER *Do your friends pressure you to drink alcohol? Learn why you need to know your limits.*

WHAT DO YOU THINK?

● Even though you know the dangers, why might you still be tempted to smoke?

● What has convinced you that smoking is a bad idea?

⁘ what tobacco does to your body

Look at the healthy people portrayed in cigarette ads; then compare those images with what smoking actually does to your body.

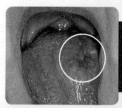

Mouth and throat Can cause cancer

Cancerous tongue

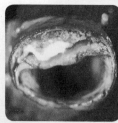

Heart Hardens and narrows arteries, starves the heart of oxygen, and increases the risk of heart disease by up to four times

Clogged artery

Lungs Destroys air sacs, inflames airways, and increases the risk of developing lung cancer by up to 23 times

Smoker's lung

Brain Increases the risk of stroke by up to four times

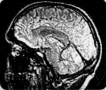

Skin Can cause premature aging

Teeth Causes discoloration

Kidneys Causes cancer

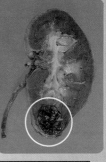

Stomach Causes cancer

Pancreas Causes cancer

Bladder Causes cancer

34

What's wrong with binge drinking?

How would you answer the following questions?
Place a ✔ in the box next to your response.

Do any of your peers engage in
underage or binge drinking? ❏ Yes ❏ No

Have your peers ever pressured
you to drink alcohol? ❏ Yes ❏ No

Have you ever been involved
in binge drinking? ❏ Yes ❏ No

WHAT is binge drinking? Some define it as simply drinking to get drunk. A report by the U.S. National Institute on Alcohol Abuse and Alcoholism tried to be more specific. It said that binge drinking is "typically defined as consuming five or more drinks in a row for men, and four or more drinks in a row for women."

If you have been tempted either to drink to excess or to drink in spite of being under the legal age, you're not alone. Many youths abuse alcohol.* But ask yourself, 'What do I really know about why I want to drink and what effects alcohol can have on me?' For example, how would you answer these true-or-false questions? Place a ✔ in the box next to your response, and then consider the facts.

a. Teens drink only because they like the taste of alcohol. ❏ True ❏ False

b. Because they are younger and fitter, teens face fewer bad side effects from alcohol abuse than do adults. ❏ True ❏ False

c. Binge drinking can't kill you. ❏ True ❏ False

d. The Bible condemns all use of alcohol. ❏ True ❏ False

e. Poor health is the only consequence of binge drinking. ❏ True ❏ False

a. Teens drink only because they like the taste of alcohol. **Answer—False.** In an alcohol-awareness survey taken in Australia, 36 percent of the young ones questioned said that they drank primarily to fit in at social activities. In the United States, a survey found that 66 percent said that they drank because of peer pressure. However, more than half also said that they drank to try to forget problems.

_____
* See the box "Who Are Doing It?" on page 249.

"A drunkard . . . will come to poverty."
—Proverbs 23:21.

• • • • • • • • •

b. Because they are younger and fitter, teens face fewer bad side effects from alcohol abuse than do adults. **Answer—False.** "New research suggests that young drinkers are courting danger," says an article in *Discover* magazine. Why? "Teens who drink excessively may be destroying significant amounts of mental capacity."

Chronic alcohol consumption is also associated with increased acne, premature wrinkling of the skin, weight gain, alcohol dependency, and drug addiction. It can also wreak havoc on the nervous system, the liver, and the heart.

c. Binge drinking can't kill you. **Answer—False.** Excessive amounts of alcohol deprive the brain of oxygen; vital bodily functions can begin to shut down. Symptoms may include vomiting, unconsciousness, and slow or irregular breathing. In some cases death can result.

d. The Bible condemns all use of alcohol. **Answer—False.** The Bible does not condemn drinking alcohol, nor is it against young people having a good time. (Psalm 104:15; Ecclesiastes 10:19) Of course, you need to be of legal age to drink.—Romans 13:1.

However, the Bible does warn against *over*drinking. "Wine is a ridiculer, intoxicating liquor is boisterous, and everyone going astray by it is not wise," says Proverbs 20:1. Alcohol can make you act in a ridiculous way! True, it may mo-

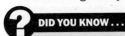

? DID YOU KNOW . . .

According to one U.S. study, "frequent binge drinkers were eight times more likely than non-binge drinkers to miss a class, fall behind in schoolwork, get hurt or injured, and damage property."

·: who are doing it?

According to a study of secondary-school children in England, Scotland, and Wales, up to one fourth of 13- and 14-year-olds "claimed to have 'downed' at least five alcoholic drinks in a single session." About half of all 15- and 16-year-olds surveyed said that they had done the same. According to the U.S. Department of Health and Human Services, "about 10.4 million adolescents ages 12 to 20 reported using alcohol. Of those, 5.1 million were binge drinkers and included 2.3 million heavy drinkers who binged at least five times a month." A study done in Australia revealed that more girls than boys in that land binge drink—consuming between 13 and 30 drinks a session!

mentarily bring you pleasure, but if you overindulge, it "bites just like a serpent," leaving you with a host of problems. —Proverbs 23:32.

e. Poor health is the only consequence of binge drinking. **Answer—False.** If you become drunk, you make yourself more vulnerable to all kinds of assault—even rape. At the same time, you might well become a danger to others, acting in a way that is completely out of character for you. The Bible warns that if you overdrink, "you will not be able to think or speak clearly." (Proverbs 23:33, *Today's English Version*) In short, you'll make yourself look foolish!

> **TIP** ✔
>
> Identify the reasons why you want to drink alcohol. Then try to think of alternative, healthier ways that you can enjoy yourself or calm distressed feelings.

> **When schoolmates offer me alcohol, I tell them that I don't need to drink to have a good time.** —Mark

Other painful consequences can include ruined friendships, poor performance at school and work, a criminal record, and poverty.—Proverbs 23:21.

Most important, consider the spiritual damage over-drinking can cause. Jehovah God wants you to serve him with "your whole mind"—not a mind needlessly damaged by overindulgence in alcohol. (Matthew 22:37) God's Word condemns not only "excesses with wine" but also "drinking matches." (1 Peter 4:3) Therefore, engaging in binge drinking runs counter to the will of our Creator and will prevent you from enjoying a close friendship with God.

What Choice Will You Make?

Will you simply follow your peers who abuse alcohol? "Do you not know," states the Bible, "that if you keep presenting yourselves to anyone as slaves to obey him, you are slaves of him because you obey him?" (Romans 6:16) Do you really want to become a slave either to your peers or to alcohol?

⟫⟫⟫ action plan!

If my peers want me to abuse alcohol with them, I will say

✎ ....

....

What I would like to ask my parent(s) about this subject is

....

....

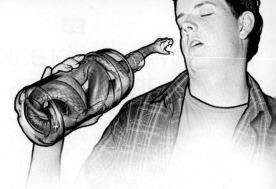

Alcohol can bite like a snake

What should you do if binge drinking has caught you in its snare? Get help immediately by speaking to a parent or a mature friend. Go to Jehovah God in prayer, and beg for his help. After all, he is "a help that is readily to be found during distresses." (Psalm 46:1) Since binge drinking and underage drinking often result from peer pressure, you may need to make substantial changes in your choice of friends.* Making such changes won't be easy, but with Jehovah's help you can succeed.

---

* For more information, see Chapters 8 and 9 of this book and Chapter 15 of Volume 2.

IN OUR NEXT CHAPTER *Drug addiction can be beaten. Find out how.*

WHAT DO YOU THINK?

- Why do your peers want others to join them in abusing alcohol?
- Will abusing alcohol make you attractive to the opposite sex, and why do you answer that way?

35

How can I break free from drugs?

ARE YOU hooked on drugs? You may know that your addiction is damaging your mind and body. You may even have tried to break the habit but then relapsed. If so, don't despair. Others have overcome drug addiction, and so can you! For example, consider what three people from very different backgrounds say about how they broke free.

NAME Marta

MY BACKGROUND My mom wasn't married when she gave birth to me, so my sister and I were brought up without a father. From about age 12, I started going to discos with an aunt who loved to dance. I was very outgoing and soon became involved with people who had bad habits. I began experimenting with drugs at the age of 13. I also started using cocaine. At first, I enjoyed using the drug. But after a while, I began having hallucinations and became afraid of everything. And when the effects of the drugs wore off, thoughts of suicide filled my mind. I wanted to quit drugs but didn't have the willpower.

HOW I BROKE FREE I began thinking about God and even attended church a few times. But I only felt more despondent. At the age of 18, I went to live with my boyfriend and had a baby. Having a son increased my desire to change my lifestyle. A former friend moved into the house opposite

> ❝ **By living up to the Bible's high standards, I have now found happiness and meaning in life.** ❞ —Marta

where I was living. She visited me and asked how I was doing. I just poured my heart out to her. She said that she had become one of Jehovah's Witnesses and offered to study the Bible with me. I accepted.

I learned that my lifestyle was not pleasing to God and that I had to quit taking drugs and smoking. But the drugs had a strong hold on me. I begged Jehovah God several times a day to help me break free from my bad habits. I wanted to please him. (Proverbs 27:11) After six months of studying the Bible and associating with Jehovah's Witnesses, I was able to quit drugs. Now my life is more meaningful. I'm no longer depressed all the time. I met a wonderful Christian man and married him. I have raised my son according to Bible principles. I am so thankful that Jehovah heard my prayers and helped me!

NAME Marcio

MY BACKGROUND I grew up on the outskirts of Santo André, a densely populated city in the state of São Paulo, Brazil. I was introduced to tobacco, drugs, and robbery at an early age. Several of my friends were involved in car theft and drug trafficking. One of them offered free drugs to youths in our area. Once they were hooked, they had to buy the drugs from him.

The police were always patrolling our area, and I was arrested a number of times for petty offenses and once on suspicion of drug trafficking.

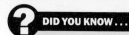
Many times I stored a gang's stolen goods and guns in my house.

People were afraid of me. My eyes were bloodshot. I never smiled. In fact, I constantly wore a murderous expression on my face. I was nicknamed "Tufão" (Typhoon) because wherever I went, I caused trouble. I also drank heavily and led an immoral life. Many of my friends died or ended up in jail. I was so down that I tied a rope around a tree branch and tried to hang myself.

HOW I BROKE FREE FROM DRUGS I asked God to help me. Eventually, I met Jehovah's Witnesses and began studying the Bible. I learned that God has a personal name, Jehovah, and that he cares about and helps those who try hard to live by his standards. (Psalm 83:18; 1 Peter 5:6, 7) I had a lot of changes to make. One of the hardest was learning to smile.

I constantly asked Jehovah for help, and I applied the Bible's advice. For example, I stopped associating with my former "friends" and avoided going to bars. Instead, I chose to associate with people who lived by Bible standards. It has been a difficult struggle, but I am no longer a thief and a troublemaker. And for more than a decade now, I have remained drug free.

NAME *Craig*

MY BACKGROUND I was raised on a farm in South Australia. My father was an alcoholic, and he and my mother separated when I was eight. My mother remarried, and I stayed with her

"Jehovah is my strength and my might."
—Isaiah 12:2.

· · · · · · · · ·

until I was 17. That year I learned to shear sheep and started living with gangs of shearers who traveled about for work. I began taking a number of different drugs and abusing alcohol. I grew my hair long. Then I waxed and plaited it and wove beads into it. I became jealous and abusive and developed a bad temper. On more than one occasion, I landed in jail.

I moved to a small town in Western Australia and lived with my girlfriend, who was a barmaid at the local hotel. We both smoked and drank, and we grew our own marijuana crop.

HOW I BROKE FREE FROM DRUGS
We had just harvested our marijuana when Jehovah's Witnesses knocked at the door of our run-down old house. I didn't merely accept what they said. Instead, over time, I proved to myself that what the Bible says is true. Then, one

TIP

If possible, avoid people, places, and things associated with your former drug use. Research shows that just seeing any of those can trigger cravings.

action plan!

If I have a relapse, I will

....

....

What I would like to ask my parent(s) about this subject is

....

....

Overcoming addiction is like escaping a burning house—you will leave things behind, but you will save your life

step at a time, I battled each of my problems.

I soon knew I had to break my marijuana habit. What would that involve? I had put a lot of effort into growing my crop, so at first I thought of giving it away. But I decided that this was not a good solution and destroyed the crop instead. Prayer played a major role in helping me overcome my drug and alcohol abuse. I asked for God's spirit to help me fight and win the battles I faced. I also stopped associating with the people who encouraged my bad habits. As I learned and applied the Bible's teachings, I gained the emotional security I needed to overcome some of my personality flaws. My girlfriend also studied the Bible and changed her habits and lifestyle. We married. For 21 years we have enjoyed better health, and we now have the pleasure of raising two children. I shudder to think what my life would be like if I hadn't had Jehovah's help in changing my lifestyle.

WHAT DO YOU THINK?

● Why might a person need to make drastic changes in his lifestyle if he wants to break free from drugs?

● How can learning the truth about God help?

Write about reasons why you think you might be tempted to smoke, binge drink, or take drugs.

Describe ways that you could enjoy yourself or calm distressed feelings without resorting to self-destructive behavior.

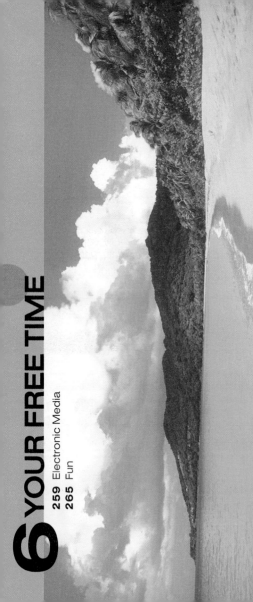

6 YOUR FREE TIME

36

Am I addicted to electronic media?

"I love, love, love texting! I think it's the greatest thing ever. I guess you could say that it has taken over my life."—Alan.

WHEN your parents entered their teens, TV and radio were the main forms of electronic media. Back then, phones were just phones—they carried only voice transmissions and had to be connected to a wall outlet. Does that sound hopelessly old-fashioned? A girl named Anna would say so. "My parents grew up in the technological dark ages," she says. "They're just now figuring out how to use some of the features on their cell phone!"

Today you can take a call, listen to music, watch a show, play a game, e-mail your friends, take a picture, and access the Internet—all on a single device you can carry in your pocket. Because you've grown up with computers, cell phones, TV, and the Internet, you may think nothing of using them all the time. Your parents, though, may feel that you're addicted. If they express concern, don't write off their comments as being out of touch with reality. "When anyone is replying to a matter before he hears it," said wise King Solomon, "that is foolishness on his part."—Proverbs 18:13.

Do you wonder why your parents might be concerned? Take the test below to see if you show signs of addiction to some form of electronic media.

Test Yourself—'Am I Addicted?'

One encyclopedia defines addiction as "habitual repetition of excessive behavior that a person is unable or unwilling to stop, despite its harmful consequences." Look at the breakdown of that definition below. Read the quotes, and see if you have said or done anything similar. Then fill in your answers.

Excessive behavior. *"I would spend hours playing electronic games. They robbed me of sleep and dominated my conversations with others. I isolated myself from my family and became lost in the imaginary worlds of the games I played."—Andrew.*

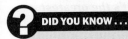

DID YOU KNOW...

Any pictures of yourself or comments about your activities that you post on a Web site today may still be accessible by potential employers and others many years from now.

In your opinion, how much time each day is it reasonable to spend using electronic media? ✎ ....

"Do not become wise in your own eyes. Fear Jehovah and turn away from bad."
—Proverbs 3:7.

• • • • • • • •

How much time do your parents think you should spend? ✎ ....

What is the *total* amount of time each day that you actually spend texting, watching TV, uploading pictures and comments onto a Web site, playing electronic games, and so on? ....

After looking at your answers above, would you say that your use of electronic media is excessive?   ❏ Yes ❏ No

Unable or unwilling to stop. *"My parents see me texting all the time and tell me that I'm doing it too much. But compared to other kids my age, I hardly text at all. I mean, compared to my parents, sure, I text more than they do. But that's like comparing apples to oranges—they're 40 and I'm 15."*—Alan.

Have your parents or friends said that you spend too much time on some form of electronic media?   ❏ Yes ❏ No

Have you been unwilling or unable to limit your use of that form of media?

❏ Yes ❏ No

Harmful consequences. *"My friends text all the time —even while driving. How unsafe is that!"*—Julie.

"When I first got my cell phone, I was always calling someone or texting someone. It was all I did. It damaged my

> **TIP**
>
> To control your use of the phone, let your friends know that you have blackout times when you will not immediately answer text messages, e-mails, or phone calls.

> **Several things helped me to overcome my addiction to TV. I forced myself to limit the amount of time I spent. I constantly talked with my mom about my problem. And I prayed a lot too.** —*Kathleen*

relationship with my family and even with some of my friends. Now I notice that when I'm out with my friends and talking to them, they constantly interrupt and say: 'Oh, hold on. I have to answer a text message.' That's one reason I'm not closer to those friends."—*Shirley.*

Do you ever read text messages or send them while driving, when in class, or during Christian meetings?
✎ ❑ Yes ❑ No

When you are conversing with family or friends, do you constantly interrupt to answer e-mails, phone calls, or text messages? ❑ Yes ❑ No

Is your use of electronic media stealing time from needed sleep or distracting you from studying? ❑ Yes ❑ No

Can you see the need to make some changes? If so, consider the following suggestions.

How to Be Balanced

If you use some form of electronic media—whether a computer, a cell phone, or another device—ask yourself the four questions below. Applying the Bible-based advice and following a few simple dos and don'ts will help you to stay safe and in control.

● **What is the content?** "Fill your minds with those things that are good and that deserve praise: things that are true, noble, right, pure, lovely, and honorable."—Philippians 4:8, *Today's English Version.*

READ MORE ABOUT THIS TOPIC IN VOLUME 2, CHAPTER 30

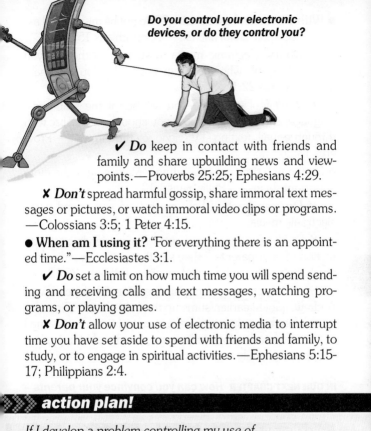

Do you control your electronic devices, or do they control you?

✔ *Do* keep in contact with friends and family and share upbuilding news and viewpoints.—Proverbs 25:25; Ephesians 4:29.

✘ *Don't* spread harmful gossip, share immoral text messages or pictures, or watch immoral video clips or programs.—Colossians 3:5; 1 Peter 4:15.

● **When am I using it?** "For everything there is an appointed time."—Ecclesiastes 3:1.

✔ *Do* set a limit on how much time you will spend sending and receiving calls and text messages, watching programs, or playing games.

✘ *Don't* allow your use of electronic media to interrupt time you have set aside to spend with friends and family, to study, or to engage in spiritual activities.—Ephesians 5:15-17; Philippians 2:4.

▶▶▶ action plan!

If I develop a problem controlling my use of

✎ ...., *I will resolve to spend*

only .... *a week using this form of media.*

What I would like to ask my parent(s) about this subject is

....

....

● **With whom am I associating?** "Do not be misled. Bad associations spoil useful habits."—1 Corinthians 15:33.

✔ *Do* use electronic media to strengthen the ties you have with people who encourage you to develop good habits.—Proverbs 22:17.

✘ *Don't* fool yourself—you will adopt the standards, language, and thinking of those you choose to socialize with through e-mail, texting, TV, video, or the Internet.—Proverbs 13:20.

● **How much time am I spending?** "Make sure of the more important things."—Philippians 1:10.

✔ *Do* keep track of how much time you spend using electronic media.

✘ *Don't* ignore the comments of your friends or the direction of your parents if they say that you're spending too much time with some form of media.—Proverbs 26:12.

Speaking of using electronic media in a balanced way, Andrew, quoted earlier, sums up the matter well: "Electronics are fun, but only for a brief amount of time. I've learned not to allow technology to become a wedge that separates me from my family and friends."

IN OUR NEXT CHAPTER *How can you convince your parents to let you have some fun?*

WHAT DO YOU THINK?

● Why might it be difficult for you to see that you are addicted to some form of electronic media?

● What might happen if you fail to control your use of electronic media?

37

Why won't my parents let me have fun?

For Allison, a teenager in Australia, Monday morning at school is as stressful as it is predictable.

"Everyone talks about what they did on the weekend," she says. "They tell stories that sound so exciting, like about how many parties they went to and how many boys they kissed—even about running away from the police . . . It sounds so scary, but fun! They come home at five o'clock in the morning, and their parents don't care. I have to be in bed before they even start their night!

"Anyway, after telling me their weekend action stories, my classmates ask me what I did. . . . I went to Christian meetings. I engaged in the ministry. I feel like I really missed out on a good time. So I usually just tell them that I did nothing. Then they ask why I didn't come with them.

"Once Mondays are over, you'd think it would be easier. But it's not. By Tuesday, everyone is talking about the upcoming weekend! I usually sit and just listen to them talk. I feel so left out!"

IS YOUR Monday morning at school similar? You might feel that there's a world of fun outside your door but that your parents have locked it tight—or as if you're at an amusement park but you're not allowed to get on any of the rides. It's not that you want to do everything your peers do. You'd just like to have fun once in a while! For example, which recreational activity would *you* most like to engage in this coming weekend?

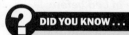

❏ dancing   ❏ music concert   ❏ other
❏ party   ❏ movie   ....

You need recreation. In fact, your Creator wants you to enjoy your youth. (Ecclesiastes 3:1, 4) And although you may doubt it at times, your parents also want you to have fun. Likely, however, your parents will have two legitimate concerns: (1) what you will do and (2) who will accompany you.

What, though, if you're invited to go out with friends but you aren't sure how your parents will react? Consider three options and their consequences.

OPTION A DON'T ASK—JUST GO

Why you might consider this option: You want to impress your friends with how independent you are. You feel that you know better than your parents, or you have little respect for their judgment. —Proverbs 14:18.

? DID YOU KNOW . . .

Loving parents will err on the side of caution. If they don't understand what you are asking for or if they feel that vital facts are missing from your request, chances are they will say no.

The consequences: Your friends may be impressed, but they'll also learn something about you—that you're deceitful. If you'd deceive your parents, you might be willing to

"Be wise, my son, and make my heart rejoice."—Proverbs 27:11.

• • • • • • • • •

deceive your friends. If your parents find out, they'll feel hurt and betrayed, and you'll likely be grounded! Disobeying your parents and going out anyhow is a foolish option. —Proverbs 12:15.

OPTION B DON'T ASK—DON'T GO

Why you might consider this option: You think about the offer and decide that the activity doesn't measure up to your principles or that some of those invited wouldn't be good company. (1 Corinthians 15:33; Philippians 4:8) On the other hand, you might want to go but don't have the courage to ask your parents.

The consequences: If you don't go because you know it's a bad idea, you'll be more confident when answering your friends. But if you don't go simply because you lack the courage to ask your parents, you might end up sitting home brooding, feeling that you're the only one who's not having fun.

OPTION C ASK—AND SEE

Why you might consider this option: You recognize your parents' authority over you and respect their judgment. (Colossians 3:20) You love your parents and don't want to hurt them by sneaking out behind their backs. (Proverbs 10:1) You also have a chance to present your case.

TIP

When going to a gathering, have an exit plan. Before you attend, know what you will do or say so that, if you need to, you can leave with your conscience intact.

> *I was so dumb when I was younger. Some of the 'fun' things I did were not so much fun in the long run. Your actions will catch up with you. I regret not listening to my parents.*
> —Brian

The consequences: Your parents feel that you love and respect them. And if they view your request as reasonable, they might say yes.

Why Parents Might Say No

What, though, if your parents say no? That can be frustrating. However, understanding their point of view may help you cope with the restrictions. For example, they might say no for one or more of the following reasons.

Greater knowledge and experience. If you had a choice, likely you would prefer to swim at a beach that is manned by lifeguards. Why? Because while you're in the water having fun, your awareness of danger is very limited. But the lifeguards have a better vantage point from which to spot hazards.

Similarly, because of their greater knowledge and experience, your parents may be aware of dangers that you do not see. Like the lifeguards on the beach, your parents' goal is, not to spoil your fun, but to help you avoid dangers that could rob you of enjoyment in life.

Love for you. Your parents have a strong desire to protect you. Love moves them to say yes when they can but no when they have to. When you ask their permission to do something, they ask *themselves* if they can grant the request and then live with the consequences. They will say yes to themselves—and to you—only if they are reasonably convinced that no harm will come to you.

READ MORE ABOUT THIS TOPIC IN VOLUME 2, CHAPTER 32

Like lifeguards on a beach, your parents have a better vantage point from which to see danger

How to Improve Your Chances of Getting a Yes

Four factors come into play.

Honesty: First, you need to ask yourself honestly: 'Why do I really want to go? Is it primarily the activity that I enjoy, or is it that I want to fit in with my peers? Is it because someone that I'm attracted to will be there?' Then be honest with your parents. They were young once, and they know you well. So they will likely discern your real motives anyhow. They'll appreciate your candor, and you'll benefit from their wisdom. (Proverbs 7:1, 2) On the other hand, if you're not honest, you undermine your credibility and lessen the chances that you'll hear a yes.

⟩⟩⟩ action plan!

If my conscience is bothered by what I see or hear when I'm at a movie or a gathering, I will

....

....

What I would like to ask my parent(s) about this subject is

....

....

Timing: Don't pummel your parents with requests when they have just arrived home from work or when they are concentrating on other matters. Approach them when they are more relaxed. But don't wait until the last minute and then try to pressure them for an answer. Your parents will not appreciate having to make a rushed decision. Ask early, giving them time to think, and your parents will appreciate your consideration.

Content: Don't be vague. Explain exactly what you want to do. Parents feel uncomfortable with the answer "I don't know," especially when they've asked you: "Who will be there?" "Will a responsible adult be present?" or "When will the event end?"

Attitude: Don't view your parents as enemies. View them as part of your team—because, all things considered, they *are*. If you view your parents as allies, you're less likely to sound combative and they are more likely to be cooperative. Avoid such statements as "You don't trust me," "Everybody else is going," or "My friends' parents are letting *them* go!" Show your parents that you're mature enough to accept their decision and respect it. If you do, they will respect you. And next time, they may be more inclined to look for ways to say yes.

WHAT DO YOU THINK?

- Why might you be reluctant to give your parents all the information they need in order to make a decision?

- What might be the consequences of your getting a yes from your parents by withholding vital facts?

Describe a recent incident when your parent said no to your request to enjoy some type of fun, and write down what you think motivates your parents to say no to you at times.

_____

_____

_____

_____

_____

List some things you learned in this section that could help improve your chances of having your parents say yes more often.

_____

_____

_____

_____

_____

_____

_____

_____

38

How can I make worship of God enjoyable?

Josh, 16, is sprawled on his bed. His mom stands at the doorway. "Joshua, get up!" she says sternly. "You *know* it's a meeting night!" Josh is being raised as one of Jehovah's Witnesses, and attendance at Christian meetings is a part of the family routine. Lately, though, Josh hasn't felt inclined to attend.

"Oh, Mom," he groans, "do I *really* have to go?"

"Stop complaining and get dressed," she replies. "I don't want to be late again!" She turns and starts to walk away.

"Look, Mom," Josh blurts out while she's still within earshot. "This may be *your* religion, but that doesn't mean it's *mine*." He knows his mom heard that because the sound of her footsteps has stopped. Then, without responding, she continues walking away.

Josh feels a twinge of guilt. He doesn't really *want* to hurt his mom. But he doesn't want to apologize either. The only thing he can do is . . .

With a sigh, Josh starts getting dressed. Then he says, more to himself than to his mom: "Sooner or later I'm going to have to make my own decision. I'm not like the others at the Kingdom Hall. I'm just not cut out to be a Christian!"

HAVE you ever felt the way Josh does in the preceding scenario? At times, does it seem that while others enjoy Christian activities, you're just going through the motions? For instance:

● Is studying the Bible just like another homework assignment to you?

● Do you dislike taking part in the door-to-door ministry?

● Do you often find yourself getting bored at Christian meetings?

If your answer is yes, don't be discouraged. You can learn to enjoy serving God. Let's see how.

CHALLENGE 1 **Studying the Bible**

Why it's not easy. Maybe you feel you're just not the "studying type." Your attention span seems short—it's *hard* to sit still and concentrate! Besides, don't you have enough studying to do for school?

Why you should do it. Not only is the Bible inspired of God but it's also "useful for teaching and helping people and for correcting them and showing them how to live." (2 Timothy 3:16, *Contemporary English Version*) Studying the Bible and meditating on what you read can open up a whole new world for you. Let's face it, nothing worthwhile comes to you without some hard work. If you want to play a sport well, you've got to learn the rules and practice the game. If you want to get fit, you need to exercise. Likewise, if you want to learn about your Creator, you need to study God's Word.

What your peers say. *"I came to a crossroads in my life when I got to high school. The kids were doing all sorts of wrong things,*

> **"Be transformed by making your mind over, that you may prove to yourselves the good and acceptable and perfect will of God."**
> —Romans 12:2.

• • • • • • • •

and I had to make some decisions: 'Is that what I want to do? Are my parents really teaching me the truth?' I had to find out for myself."—Tshedza.

"I always believed that what I had learned was the truth, but I needed to prove it to myself. I had to make it my own religion—as opposed to it being just a family religion."—Nelisa.

What you can do. Make up your own, customized personal study plan. *You* get to choose which subjects you'll explore. Where could you start? Why not dig into your Bible and scrutinize your beliefs, perhaps using a book such as *What Does the Bible Really Teach?**

Get started! Put a ✔ next to two or three Bible topics below that you'd like to learn more about—or, if you prefer, write in some of your own.

❏ Is there a God?
❏ How can I be sure that the Bible writers were inspired by God?

---

* Published by Jehovah's Witnesses.

If you want to become physically fit, you need to exercise. If you want to become spiritually fit, you need to study God's Word

- ❏ Why should I believe in creation rather than evolution?
- ❏ What is God's Kingdom, and how can I prove its existence?
- ❏ How can I explain my belief about what happens at death?
- ❏ Why should I be convinced that there will be a resurrection?
- ❏ How can I be sure which is the true religion?

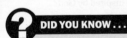

....

....

....

CHALLENGE 2 **Engaging in the Ministry**

Why it's not easy. Talking to others about the Bible —or encountering a schoolmate while doing so—can be scary.

Why you should do it. Jesus instructed his followers: "Make disciples . . . , teaching them to observe all the things I have commanded you." (Matthew 28:19, 20) But there are further reasons for doing it. Studies suggest that in some places the vast majority of teens believe in God and in the Bible. Yet, those same youths have no genuine hope for the future. Through your study of the Bible, you have the very information that many of your peers are searching for and need! By sharing your beliefs with others, you will feel better about yourself, and more important, you will make Jehovah's heart rejoice.—Proverbs 27:11.

What your peers say. *"My friend and I prepared effective introductions, and we learned how to overcome objections and how to make return visits. Once I started putting more into my ministry, it became more enjoyable."* —Nelisa.

"One Christian sister has helped me out so much! She's six years older than I am, and she takes me out in the ministry with her and sometimes out to breakfast. She showed me encouraging scriptures that helped me to rearrange my thinking. I find that now I reach out to people more because of her wonderful example. I could never repay her!" —Shontay.

What you can do. With your parents' permission, find someone in your congregation who is older than you and with whom you can share in the ministry. (Acts 16:1-3) The Bible states: "By iron, iron itself is sharpened. So one man sharpens the face of another." (Proverbs 27:17) There are many benefits to associating with older ones who have a wealth of experience. "It's actually a relief to be around older ones," says 19-year-old Alexis.

Get started! Below, write the name of someone in your congregation in addition to your parents who could assist you in the ministry.

✎ ....

CHALLENGE 3 Attending Christian Meetings

Why it's not easy. After sitting in class all day, an hour or so of listening to Bible-based talks might seem like an eternity.

Why you should do it. The Bible exhorts Christians: "Let us consider one another to incite to love and fine works, not forsaking the gathering of ourselves together, as some have the custom, but encouraging one another,

> **The religion I'm in is no longer just my parents' religion but my religion. Jehovah is my God, and I don't want to do anything that will harm my relationship with him.**
> —Samantha

and all the more so as you behold the day drawing near."
—Hebrews 10:24, 25.

What your peers say. "Preparing for congregation meetings is an absolute must. Sometimes you just have to motivate yourself. When you do prepare, you enjoy the meetings because you know what's being discussed, and you can even participate."—Elda.

"At one point, I began to notice that when I gave comments at the meetings, those meetings became much more interesting to me."—Jessica.

What you can do. Take time to prepare in advance, and if you can, offer a comment. This will help you to feel more a part of what is going on.

>>> action plan!

I will schedule .... minutes of Bible reading each day and will spend .... each week preparing for Christian meetings.

To pay better attention at Christian meetings, I will

....

....

What I would like to ask my parent(s) about this subject is

....

....

To illustrate: What's more enjoyable—watching a sport on television or playing it on the field? Obviously, being a participant is more rewarding than being a spectator. Why not take that approach to Christian meetings?

TIP ✓

Get a notebook, and start writing down main points at Christian meetings. Time will pass faster, and learning will be easier!

Get started! In the space below, write down the time when you can spend just 30 minutes each week preparing for a congregation meeting.

✎ ....

Many youths are experiencing the truthfulness of Psalm 34:8, which says: "Taste and see that Jehovah is good." How satisfying is it just to *hear* about a mouthwatering dish? Isn't it better to savor the food for yourself? It's the same with worshipping God. Taste and see for yourself how rewarding it is to participate in spiritual activities. The Bible says that the one who is not just a hearer but a doer of the work "will be happy in his doing it."—James 1:25.

IN OUR NEXT CHAPTER *Learn how to set—and reach—your goals.*

WHAT DO YOU THINK?

- **Why might spiritual activities seem boring to a teenager?**
- **Which of the three aspects of worship discussed in this chapter would you like to work on?**

⠶ they set goals

The Bible states: "You do not know what your life will be tomorrow." (James 4:14) In some cases, death comes unexpectedly and at a young age. As you read the experiences of Catrina and Kyle, note how they made a good name with Jehovah God during their brief lives by setting and reaching spiritual goals.—Ecclesiastes 7:1.

Catrina passed away at the age of 18, but at 13 she had already written out a "life plan"—a list of goals she wanted to achieve. Her goals included entering the full-time ministry, serving in a land where there is a need for Bible teachers, and working along with her dad on Kingdom Hall construction projects. She wrote: "I have made a dedication of my life to Jehovah God!" Catrina's aim was to "live according to his standards, in a way that makes him happy." At her funeral, Catrina was described as a "beautiful young woman who had her whole life planned out to be centered around Jehovah."

at right now we can set ... als" A goal is: a point set to reach for, a final purpose, some goals that Kyle can ... each are: → Contributions

Get baptised; Give Talks at the K.H...

Help build Kingdom Halls

To: Welcome to Watchtower Farms!

or to: Watchtower Educational Center

And there Kyle could work making magazines + books about Jehovah and wait for the Paradise.

From an early age, Kyle was taught to have goals. After a tragic car accident claimed his life at age 20, his relatives found a "goal book" that his mom helped him make when he was just four years old. His goals included getting baptized, giving talks at the Kingdom Hall, and serving at the headquarters of Jehovah's Witnesses, where he could assist in producing literature that would help people to learn about God. After looking through Kyle's goal book, made so many years earlier, his mother stated, "He reached every one of those goals."

What goals have *you* set for yourself? You do not know what your life will hold tomorrow. So, use each day you have to the full. Like Catrina and Kyle, spend your time in the most rewarding way possible. Imitate the apostle Paul, who could say near the close of his life: "I have fought the fine fight, I have run the course to the finish, I have observed the faith." (2 Timothy 4:7) The following chapter will help you to do just that!

39

How can I reach my goals?

Which of the following would you like to have?

- ❏ More confidence
- ❏ More friends
- ❏ More happiness

ACTUALLY, you can have *all three!* How? By setting and reaching goals. Consider the following:

More confidence. When you set small goals and reach them, you'll have the confidence to take on bigger ones. You'll also feel more confident when facing day-to-day challenges—such as standing up to peer pressure.

More friends. People enjoy being around those who are reasonably goal-oriented—those who know what they want and who are willing to work for it.

More happiness. Let's face it: There's little fun in being bored or waiting for your life to happen. On the other hand, when you set and reach goals, you feel a sense of accomplishment. Ready to get started? The following pages will help!*

---

* These suggestions are geared toward short-term goals, but the principles apply to long-range goals as well.

> *It's easy to get discouraged if you don't have anything to focus on or look forward to. But when you set and reach goals, you feel good about yourself.* —Reed

✓1 IDENTIFY

1. Brainstorm potential goals. Have fun with this step! Don't analyze; just write down as many ideas as you can. See if you can come up with at least 10 possibilities.

2. Evaluate your ideas. Which ones seem the most exciting? The most challenging? Which would you be especially proud of achieving? Remember, the best goals are often the ones that mean the most to *you*.

3. Prioritize. Number your goals according to the order in which you would like to achieve them.

Sample Goals

Friendship Make one friend outside my age group. Reestablish an old friendship.

Health Exercise at least 90 minutes each week. Get eight hours of sleep each night.

School Improve my grades in math. Stand up for what is right when pressured to do what is wrong.

Spirituality Read the Bible for 15 minutes each day. Share my beliefs with a classmate this week.

☑2 PLAN

For each of the goals you've chosen, do the following:

List your goal.

Set a deadline. After all, a goal without a deadline is just a dream!

Plan the steps involved.

Anticipate obstacles. Then think of how you'll overcome them.

Make a commitment. Promise yourself that you'll do your best to reach this goal. Now sign and date it.

 DID YOU KNOW . . .

The bigger the goal, the more satisfying your feeling of accomplishment on reaching it!

Learn Spanish for my trip to Mexico
July 1

Steps
1. Get a phrase book.
2. Learn ten new words each week.
3. Listen to other people speaking Spanish.
4. Ask someone to verify my grammar and pronunciation.

Potential obstacles
No one nearby speaks Spanish

How I can overcome them
Download audio recordings in Spanish from www.jw.org.

....

Signature   Date

Goals are like blueprints —it takes work to turn them into reality

TIP

Don't worry about rigidly sticking to a plan. Be flexible, and make adjustments as you progress toward your goal.

"The plans of the diligent one surely make for advantage."—Proverbs 21:5.

• • • • • • • •

☑3 ACT!

Start immediately. Ask yourself, 'What can I do today to start toward my goal?' Granted, you may not have every detail worked out, but don't let that keep you from getting started. As the Bible puts it, "if you wait until the wind and the weather are just right, you will never plant anything and never harvest anything." (Ecclesiastes 11:4, *Today's English Version*) Find something you can do *today*—even if it's small—and do it.

Review your goals daily. Remind yourself why each one is important to you. Track your progress by putting a ✔ (or a completed-on date) next to each step as you complete it.

Use your imagination. Think ahead and imagine yourself achieving your goal. Feel the sense of accomplishment. Next, think back through the individual steps, one at a time, and visualize each of them. Finally, see yourself completing each step, and imagine how great you'll feel when you reach your goal. Now go for it!

WHAT DO YOU THINK?

- **Is it possible to have too many goals at once?** —Philippians 1:10.

- **Does setting goals mean planning out every minute of your life?**—Philippians 4:5.

Timothy

Timothy is about to leave home—not to run away from his family but to become a missionary companion of the apostle Paul! Possibly in his late teens, Timothy is already a **responsible young man** who has been "well reported on by the brothers in Lystra and Iconium." (Acts 16:2) Paul is confident that Timothy can **accomplish great things** in God's service. And he does! In the years that follow, Timothy travels extensively, establishing congregations and building up the brotherhood. Timothy's **fine qualities** endear him to Paul, who some 11 years later tells the Philippians: "I have no one else of a disposition like his who will genuinely care for the things pertaining to you." —Philippians 2:20.

Are you **making yourself available** to be used in God's service? If you are, great blessings await you! Jehovah truly values young ones who **"offer themselves willingly."** (Psalm 110:3) Furthermore, you can be assured that Jehovah God "is not unrighteous so as to forget your work." —Hebrews 6:10.

my journal

Below, write about what convinces you that a loving God exists.

✎

_____

_____

_____

_____

_____

_____

_____

Write down two goals you would like to set with regard to your worship.

_____

_____

_____

_____

_____

_____

_____

_____

_____

QUESTIONS PARENTS ASK

"How can I get my child to talk to me?"

"Should I enforce a curfew?"

"How can I help my daughter gain a balanced view of dieting?"

Those are some of the 17 questions answered in this Appendix. The material is divided into six sections and cross-indexed to the appropriate chapters in both Volume 1 and Volume 2 of *Questions Young People Ask—Answers That Work*.

Read the material. If possible, discuss it with your spouse. Then use the advice in helping your children. The answers you will find here are trustworthy. They are based, not on fallible human wisdom, but on God's Word, the Bible.—2 Timothy 3: 16, 17.

COMMUNICATION

Is there really any harm in arguing with either my spouse or my children?

In marriage, disagreements are inevitable. How you handle them, though, is a matter of choice. Youths are profoundly affected by their parents' arguments. This is a matter of concern, since your marriage is, in effect, a model that your children are likely to follow if they marry. Why not use disagreements as an opportunity to demonstrate effective ways to resolve conflicts? Try the following:

SEE VOLUME 1, CHAPTER 2, AND VOLUME 2, CHAPTER 24

Listen. The Bible tells us to be "swift about hearing, slow about speaking, slow about wrath." (James 1:19) Don't add fuel to the fire by 'returning evil for evil.' (Romans 12:17) Even if your spouse seems unwilling to listen, *you* can choose to do so.

Strive to explain rather than criticize. In a calm manner, tell your spouse how his or her conduct has affected you. ("I feel hurt when you . . .") Resist the urge to accuse and criticize. ("You don't care about me." "You never listen.")

Take a time-out. Sometimes it is best to drop the matter and resume the discussion when tempers have cooled down. The Bible says: "The beginning of contention is as one letting out waters; so before the quarrel has burst forth, take your leave."—Proverbs 17:14.

Apologize to each other—and, if appropriate, to your children. Brianne, 14, says: "Sometimes after they've argued, my parents will apologize to me and my older brother because they know how it affects us." One of the most valuable lessons you can teach your children is how to say humbly, "I'm sorry."

What, though, if the problem involves arguing with your children? Consider if you are unwittingly adding fuel to the fire. For instance, look at the scenario that opens Chapter 2 on page 15 of this volume. Can you identify some things Rachel's mom did that contributed to the argument? How can you avoid arguing with your teen? Try the following:

● Avoid sweeping assertions, such as "You always . . ." or "You never . . ." Such statements only invite a defensive response. After all, they are likely to be exaggerations, and your child knows it. Your child may also know that sweeping assertions are really more about your anger than his or her irresponsibility.

● Rather than using blunt statements that begin with the word "you," try expressing how your child's behavior affects you. For example, "I feel . . . when you . . ." Believe it or not, deep down, your feelings are important to your teen. By letting your teen know how you are affected, you are more likely to elicit his or her cooperation.*

● Hard as it may be, hold back until your temper is in check. (Proverbs 29:22) If the issue that is causing the argument involves chores, discuss it with your child. Write down specifically what is required of him or her, and if necessary, make clear what the consequences will be if your expectations are not met. Patiently listen to your child's point of view, even if you feel that view is incorrect. Most teens respond better to a listening ear than to a lecture.

---

* At the same time, do not use guilt to motivate your adolescent.

● Before hastily concluding that a spirit of rebellion has taken control of your teen, realize that much of what you observe is part of your child's natural development. Your child may argue a point just to prove that he is growing up. Resist the urge to get involved in disputes. Remember, how you respond to provocation teaches a lesson to your teen. Set an example in patience and long-suffering, and your son or daughter will likely imitate you.—Galatians 5: 22, 23.

How much should my children know about my past?

Imagine yourself in this situation: You're eating dinner with your spouse, your daughter, and some family friends. During the conversation, your friend mentions someone whom you dated—and broke up with—before meeting your spouse. Your daughter nearly drops her fork. "You mean you dated someone else?" she gasps. You haven't shared this story with your daughter before. Now she wants to know more. What will you do?

SEE VOLUME 1, CHAPTER 1

Usually, it's best to welcome your child's questions. After all, anytime that he or she is asking questions and listening to your answers is time that you're communicating —something most parents desire.

Just how much should you tell your son or daughter about your past? Naturally, you might prefer to withhold embarrassing information. Yet, where appropriate, revealing some of your struggles can be helpful to your children. How so?

Consider an example. The apostle Paul once disclosed about himself: "When I wish to do what is right, what is bad is present with me. . . . Miserable man that I am!" (Romans 7:21-24) Jehovah God inspired those words to be recorded and preserved in the Bible for our benefit. And we do indeed benefit, for who cannot relate to Paul's candid expression?

Similarly, hearing about your good choices *and* your mistakes can help your children relate to you better. Granted, you were raised in a different era. However, while times have changed, human nature has not; neither have Scriptural principles. (Psalm 119:144) Discussing challenges you've faced—and how you overcame them—can help your teenagers as they work through *their* problems. "When you discover that your parents have faced challenges similar to your own, it makes your parents seem a lot more real," says a young man named Cameron. He adds, "The next time you have a problem, you wonder if your parents have been through *this* before too."

A caution: Not all stories necessarily need to end with counsel. True, you might be concerned that your teen will draw the wrong conclusion or even feel justified in making similar mistakes himself. But instead of summarizing what you want your child to take away from the discussion ("That's why you should never . . ."), briefly state how *you* feel. ("In hindsight, I wish I hadn't done such-and-such because . . .") Your son or daughter can thus learn a valuable lesson from your experience without feeling as if he or she has been given a lecture.—Ephesians 6:4.

How can I get my child to talk to me?

When they were little, your children probably talked to you about everything. If you asked a question, they answered without hesitation. Often, in fact, you didn't have to ask questions at all; information would gush forth like a geyser. In

SEE VOLUME 1, CHAPTERS 1 AND 2

contrast, getting your *teenagers* to talk may seem as futile as extracting water from a dry well. 'They talk to their friends,' you say to yourself. 'Why won't they talk to *me?*'

Don't let their silence cause you to conclude that your teenagers have rejected you or that they don't want you to be involved in their life. The fact is, they need you now more than ever. And the good news is, research reveals that most teenagers *still value* the advice of their parents—even over that of their peers or the media.

Then why are they so reluctant to tell you what's on their mind? Consider what some youths say about why they hold back from talking to their parents. Then ask yourself the accompanying questions and look up the cited scriptures.

> *"I find it hard to approach Dad because he has a lot on his plate, both at work and in the congregation. There never really seems to be a convenient time to talk to him."—Andrew.*

'Have I unwittingly sent the message that I'm too busy to talk to my teenagers? If so, how can I make myself more approachable? When can I set aside some time regularly to talk with my children?'—Deuteronomy 6:7.

> *"I approached my mother in tears about an argument I'd had at school. I wanted her to comfort me, but instead she just reprimanded me. Since then, I haven't approached her about anything important."—Kenji.*

'How do I respond when my children approach me with a problem? Even if correction is in order, can I learn to stop and listen with empathy before giving advice?'—James 1:19.

> *"It seems that every time parents say we can talk and they won't get angry, they still become upset. Then the teen feels betrayed."—Rachel.*

'If my child tells me something that is upsetting, how can I control my initial reaction?'—Proverbs 10:19.

"Many times when I opened up to Mom about very private matters, she turned around and told them to her friends. I lost confidence in her for a long time."
—Chantelle.

'Do I show consideration for my child's feelings by not spreading private matters that he or she has confided to me?'—Proverbs 25:9.

"I have a lot of things I want to talk about with my parents. I just need their help to start the conversation."—Courtney.

'Can I take the initiative to talk to my adolescent? What times are best for talking together?'—Ecclesiastes 3:7.

As a parent, you have everything to gain by building bridges of communication between you and your child. Consider the experience of 17-year-old Junko in Japan. "One time," she says, "I admitted to my mother that I felt more at ease with my schoolmates than with fellow Christians. The next day, there was a letter from Mom on my desk. In the letter she told me how she too had felt the lack of friends among fellow believers. She reminded me of individuals in the Bible who served God even when there wasn't anyone for them to be with who would encourage them. She also commended me for the efforts I had made to cultivate wholesome friendships. I was surprised to learn that I was not the only one who had faced this problem. My mother had too, and I was so happy to learn about it that I cried. I was very encouraged by what my mother told me, and I was strengthened to do what was right."

As Junko's mother found out, teenagers tend to open up to parents when they are assured that their thoughts and feelings will not be met with ridicule or criticism. But what can you do if your teenager seems annoyed or even angry when he or she speaks to you? Resist the urge to respond in kind. (Romans 12:21; 1 Peter 2:23) Instead, as hard as it may seem, show by example the type of speech and behavior that you expect of your teenager.

Remember this: As they grow to adulthood, teenagers are in a stage of transition. Experts have noted that during this period, adolescents tend to fluctuate in their behavior—on one occasion acting older than their years and on another occasion acting more like a child. If you notice this with your teenager, what can you do—especially on an occasion when he or she acts *younger* than his or her years?

Resist the urge to lash out in criticism or get embroiled in a childish dispute. Instead, appeal to your teenager as an "adult in training." (1 Corinthians 13:11) For example, if the childish side of your teenager emerges and he or she says, "Why are you always nagging me?" you might be tempted to respond in anger. If you do so, however, you give up control of the conversation, and you will likely become trapped in an argument. On the other hand, you could simply say: "It sounds like you're really upset. Why don't we discuss this later after you've cooled down?" That way, you stay in control. The stage is now set for a *conversation,* rather than an *argument.*

RULES

Should I enforce a curfew?

To help answer that question, imagine yourself in this situation: It's 30 minutes past your son's curfew, and you hear the front door slowly creak open. 'He hopes that I've gone to bed,' you think to yourself. You haven't, of course. In fact, you've been sitting near the door since the time your son was supposed to come home. The door is now fully open, and your son's eyes meet yours. What will you say? What will you do?

SEE VOLUME 1, CHAPTER 3, AND VOLUME 2, CHAPTER 22

You have options. You could make light of the matter. 'Boys will be boys,' you might tell yourself. Or you could swing to the other extreme and say, "You're grounded for life!" Rather than act impulsively, listen first, in case there is a valid reason for his being late. Then you can turn a broken curfew into a powerful teaching tool. How?

Suggestion: Tell your child that you will discuss the matter with him or her tomorrow. Then, at an appropriate time, sit down and talk about how you will handle the matter. Some parents have tried the following: If their son or daughter comes home after the time agreed on, then for the next outing, the curfew will be moved 30 minutes earlier. On the other hand, if the boy or girl regularly comes home on time and builds up a record of reliable behavior, you might consider granting reasonable freedoms—on occasion, perhaps even extending the curfew to a later time. It is important that your child clearly knows what time he or she is expected to be home and what consequences will be meted out for failure to abide by the curfew you have set. You then need to enforce those consequences.

Note, however, that the Bible says: "Let your reasonableness become known." (Philippians 4:5) So, before imposing a curfew, you might want to discuss the matter with your child, allowing him or her to suggest a time and offer reasons for that preference. Take this request into consideration. If your child has demonstrated himself or herself to be responsible, you might be able to accommodate his or her wishes if they are reasonable.

Punctuality is a part of life. Setting up a curfew, then, isn't just about getting your child off the streets. It's about teaching a skill that will benefit your child long after leaving home. —Proverbs 22:6.

How can I handle conflicts with my children over clothing?

Consider the opening scenario on page 77 in this volume. Imagine that Heather is your daughter. You cannot help but notice the skimpy little outfit she's wearing—a little too much of nothing, in your view. Your reaction is immediate. "Go upstairs and change, young lady, or you're not going *anywhere!*" Such a response

SEE VOLUME 1, CHAPTER 11

may well get results. After all, your daughter has little choice but to comply. But how do you teach her to change her thinking and not just her clothes?

● First, remember this: *The consequences of immodesty must matter as much or more to your adolescent than they do to you.* Deep down, your adolescent does not want to look foolish or invite unwanted attention. Patiently point out that immodest styles are really not flattering, and explain why.* Recommend alternatives.

● Second, be reasonable. Ask yourself, 'Does the garment violate a Bible principle, or is this just a matter of personal taste?' (2 Corinthians 1:24; 1 Timothy 2:9, 10) If it is a matter of taste, can you make a concession?

● Third, don't just tell your adolescent what styles are *not* acceptable. Help him or her to find clothes that *are* appropriate. Why not use the worksheets on pages 82 and 83 of this volume to help you reason with your child? It will be well worth your time and effort!

---

* Your adolescent is likely very body-conscious, so be careful not to imply that his or her body is flawed.

Should I allow my child to play electronic games?

Electronic games have come a long way since you were a teen. As a parent, how can you help your child identify the potential dangers and avoid them?

SEE VOLUME 2, CHAPTER 30
Little good will be accomplished by condemning the entire industry or by dogmatically asserting that electronic games are a complete waste of time. Remember, not *all* games are bad. However, they can be addictive. So analyze the amount of time your child spends playing these games. Also, consider the type of games to which your child seems attracted. You could even ask your child such questions as these:

● Which game is the most popular among your classmates?

● What happens in the game?

● Why do you think the game is so popular?

You might find that your child knows more about electronic games than you thought! Perhaps he or she has even played games that you feel are objectionable. If that is the case, don't overreact. This is an opportunity for you to help your child develop perceptive powers.—Hebrews 5:14.

Ask questions that will help your child determine *why* the attraction to objectionable games exists. For example, you could ask a question like this:

● Do you feel left out because you aren't allowed to play that particular game?

Some youths may play a certain game so that they will have something to talk about with their peers. If this is so in your child's case, you will likely not address the situation the way you would if you found that your child was attracted to games containing gory violence or sexual overtones. —Colossians 4:6.

But what if your child *is* attracted to the negative elements of a game? Some youths may quickly insist that they aren't affected by computer-generated gore. 'Just because I do it on screen doesn't mean I'll do it in real life,' they reason. If that's how your child feels, draw his or her attention to Psalm 11:5. As the wording of the scripture makes clear, it is not just *being* violent that merits God's disapproval but *loving* violence does too. The same principle applies to sexual immorality or any other vice that God's Word condemns.—Psalm 97:10.

If electronic games pose a problem for your child, try the following:

● Do not allow electronic games to be played in a secluded area, such as the bedroom.

● Set ground rules—for example, no games before finishing homework or dinner or some other essential activity.

RULES

● Emphasize the value of activities that require physical exertion.

● Watch your children play their electronic games—or, better yet, play with them at times.

Of course, to guide your children in the matter of content, you need to have freeness of speech. So ask yourself, 'What kind of TV shows and movies do I watch?' Make no mistake—if you have a double standard, your children will know it!

What if my child is addicted to the cell phone, the computer, or other electronic media?

Does your adolescent spend too much time online, send and receive too many text messages, or have a better relationship with his MP3 player than he has with you? If so, what can you do?

You could just take the device away from your child. But do not write off all electronic media as evil. After all, likely you use some form of electronic media that was not available to *your* parents. So instead of simply confiscating your adolescent's device—unless there is compelling reason to do so—why not use this as an opportunity to train your son or daughter to use electronic media wisely and with moderation? How can you do that?

SEE VOLUME 1, CHAPTER 36

Sit down and discuss the matter with your adolescent. First, state your concerns. Second, *listen* to what he or she has to say. (Proverbs 18:13) Third, work out practical solutions. Don't be afraid to set firm limits, but be reasonable. "When I had a problem with texting," says a teenager named Ellen, "my parents didn't take away my phone; they set guidelines. The way they handled it has helped me to be balanced in my use of texting, even when my parents aren't there to monitor me."

What if your son or daughter reacts defensively? Do not conclude that your counsel has fallen on deaf ears. Instead, be patient and give your adolescent some time to think about the matter. Chances are, he or she already agrees with you and will make needed adjustments. Many youths are similar to a teen named Hailey, who says: "At first I was offended when my parents told me I was addicted to my computer. But later, the more I thought about it, the more I realized that they were right."

INDEPENDENCE

How much independence should I allow my child?

This question may seem to get complex when you consider privacy issues. For instance, what if your son is in his bedroom with the door closed? Should you barge in without knocking? Or what if your daughter left her cell phone behind as she rushed off to school? Should you peek at her stored text messages?

SEE VOLUME 1, CHAPTERS 3 AND 15

These are not easy questions to answer. As a parent, you have a right to know what is going on in your adolescent's life and an obligation to keep him or her safe. But you cannot forever be a 'helicopter parent,' suspiciously hovering over your child and monitoring his or her every move. How can you strike a balance?

First, recognize that an adolescent's desire for privacy does not *always* spell trouble. Often, it is a normal part of growth. Privacy helps adolescents 'test their wings' as they forge their own friendships and think through their problems using their "power of reason." (Romans 12:1, 2) Privacy helps adolescents develop thinking ability—a vital quality if they are to function as responsible adults. It also gives them opportunity to meditate before making decisions or answering difficult questions.—Proverbs 15:28.

Second, realize that attempts to micromanage your adolescent's life may breed resentment and rebellion. (Ephesians 6:4; Colossians 3:21) Does this mean that you should back off? No, for you are still the parent. However, the goal is for your child to acquire a trained conscience. (Deuteronomy 6:6, 7; Proverbs 22:6) In the end, guidance is more effective than surveillance.

Third, discuss the matter with your adolescent. Listen to his or her concerns. Might there be times when you could be yielding? Let your adolescent know that you will allow him or her a measure of privacy as long as your trust is not betrayed. Outline the consequences of disobedience, and follow through if it becomes necessary. Be assured that you *can* give your adolescent some privacy without relinquishing your role as a caring parent.

INDEPENDENCE

When should my child leave school?

"My teachers are boring!" "I get too much homework!" "I struggle just to get passing grades—why even *try?*" Because of such frustrations, some youths are tempted to quit school before they have acquired the skills they will need to make a living. If your son or daughter wants to quit school, what can you do? Try the following:

SEE VOLUME 1, CHAPTER 19

● *Examine your own attitude toward education.* Did you view school as a waste of time—a 'prison sentence' that you had to endure until the day you could pursue more important goals? If so, your attitude toward learning may have rubbed off on your children. The fact is, a well-rounded education will help them acquire "practical wisdom and thinking ability"—qualities they need in order to reach their goals.—Proverbs 3:21.

● *Provide the tools.* Some who could be getting better grades simply don't know *how* to study—or they don't have the appropriate environment for it. A good study area might include an uncluttered desk with sufficient light and research tools. You can help your child to make advancement—whether secular or spiritual—by providing the right setting for pondering over new thoughts and ideas.—Compare 1 Timothy 4:15.

● *Get involved.* View teachers and guidance counselors as your allies, not your enemies. Meet them. Know their names. Talk to them about your child's goals and challenges. If your child is struggling with grades, try to determine the cause. For example, does your child feel that excelling at school will make him or her a target of bullying? Is there a problem with a teacher? What about the courses? Your child should be challenged by the curriculum, not overwhelmed by it. Another possibility: Could there be an underlying physical cause, such as poor eyesight, or a learning disability?

The more involved you are in your child's training, both secular and spiritual, the better chance your child has of success.—Psalm 127:4, 5.

How will I know when my child is ready to leave home?

Serena, quoted in Chapter 7 of this volume, fears leaving home. What is one reason? She says: "Even when I want to buy something with my own money, Dad won't let me. He says that's his job. So the idea of having to pay my own bills is scary." Serena's father no doubt means well, but do you think that he is helping to prepare his daughter to manage her own household? —Proverbs 31:10, 18, 27.

SEE VOLUME 1, CHAPTER 7

Are your children overprotected and thus underprepared to face living on their own? How can you know? Consider the following four skills, also mentioned in Chapter 7 under the subheading "Am I Prepared?"—but now do so from a parent's perspective.

Money management. Do your older children know how to fill out a tax return or what they need to do to comply with local tax laws? (Romans 13:7) Do they know how to use credit responsibly? (Proverbs 22:7) Can they budget their income and then live within their means? (Luke 14:28-30) Have they felt the pleasure that comes from acquiring an item that they bought with money they earned? Have they experienced the even greater pleasure that comes from giving of their time and resources to help others?—Acts 20:35.

Domestic skills. Do your daughters *and* sons know how to cook meals? Have you taught them how to wash and iron clothes? If they drive a car, can your children safely carry out simple maintenance, such as changing a fuse, the oil, or a flat tire?

Social skills. When your older children have disagreements, do you always act as the referee, imposing the final solution to the problem? Or have you trained your children to negotiate a peaceful solution to the problem and then report back to you?—Matthew 5:23-25.

Personal spiritual routine. Do you tell your children what they should believe, or do you persuade them? (2 Timothy 3: 14, 15) Rather than always answering their religious and moral questions, are you teaching them to develop "thinking ability"? (Proverbs 1:4) Would you want them to follow your pattern of personal Bible study, or would you want them to do something better?*

Without a doubt, training your children in the above areas takes time and considerable effort. But the rewards are well worth it when the bittersweet time comes for you to hug them good-bye.

---

* See pages 315-318.

SEX AND DATING

Should I talk to my child about sex?

The subject of sex is being introduced to children at a remarkably young age. The Bible long ago foretold that "the last days" would be marked by "critical times hard to deal with," in which people would be "without self-control" and "lovers of pleasures rather than lovers of God." (2 Timothy 3:1, 3, 4) The trend of having casual sex is one of many indications that this prophecy has proved true.

SEE VOLUME 1, CHAPTERS 23, 25, AND 32, AND VOLUME 2, CHAPTERS 4-6, 28, AND 29

The world today is vastly different from the one in which you were raised. In some ways, though, the issues are the same. So do not feel overwhelmed or intimidated by the bad influences that surround your children. Instead, be determined to help them to do as the apostle Paul urged Christians some 2,000 years ago, saying: "Put on the complete suit of armor from God that you may be able to stand firm against the machinations of the Devil." (Ephesians 6:11) The fact is, many Christian youths are putting up a commendable fight to do what is right, despite the negative influences that surround them. How can you help your children to do the same?

One way is to open a discussion, using selected chapters in Section 4 of this book and Sections 1 and 7 of

Volume 2. The chapters contain thought-provoking scriptures. Some highlight the true-life examples of those who either took a stand for what is right and reaped blessings or ignored God's laws and paid the consequences. Other scriptures contain principles that can help your children recognize the great privilege that they—and you—have of living by God's laws. Why not plan to review this material with them soon?

Should I let my child start dating?

The dating issue is certain to be thrust upon your children sooner or later. "I don't even have to do anything!" says Phillip. "Girls ask me out, and I stand there thinking, 'Oh, what am I going to do now?' It's hard to say no because some of them are very beautiful!"

SEE VOLUME 2, CHAPTERS 1-3

The best thing that you can do as parents is talk to your teen about dating, perhaps using Chapter 1 in Volume 2 as a basis for discussion. Find out how your son or daughter feels about the challenges he or she faces at school and even in the Christian congregation. Sometimes such discussions can take place on informal occasions, such as "when you sit in your house and when you walk on the road." (Deuteronomy 6:6, 7) Whatever the setting, remember to be "swift about hearing, slow about speaking."—James 1:19.

If your son or daughter expresses interest in someone of the opposite sex, don't panic. "When my dad found out that I had a boyfriend, he was so upset!" says one teenage girl. "He tried to scare me by asking me all these questions about whether I was ready for marriage—which, when you're young, can make you feel like you want to prolong the relationship and prove your parents wrong!"

If your teen knows that dating isn't even up for discussion, something tragic may happen—he or she may drive the relationship underground and date secretly. "When parents overreact," says one girl, "it only makes kids want to hide the relationship more. They don't stop. They just get sneakier."

You will get far better results by having frank discussions. Brittany, 20, says: "My parents have always been very open with me about dating. It's important for them to know whom I'm interested in, and I think that's nice! My dad will talk to the person. If there are any concerns, my parents tell me. Usually I decide I'm not interested before it even reaches the dating level."

After reading Chapter 2 in Volume 2, though, you might wonder, 'Would my son or daughter date behind my back?' Note what a number of youths say about why some are tempted to date secretly, and then think about the accompanying questions.

"Some kids aren't finding comfort at home, so they decide to lean on a boyfriend or girlfriend."—Wendy.

As a parent, how can you make sure that the emotional needs of your children are adequately cared for? Are there improvements you can make in this regard? If so, what are they?

"When I was 14, an exchange student asked me to be his girlfriend. I agreed. I thought it would be nice to have a guy put his arms around me."—Diane.

If Diane were your daughter, how would you address this issue?

"Mobile phones make secret dating easy. Parents have no idea what is going on!"—Annette.

What precautions can you take when it comes to your children's use of cell phones?

"Secret dating is much easier when parents don't keep a close enough eye on what their children are doing and with whom."—Thomas.

Are there ways you can be more a part of your teenager's life and still allow him or her appropriate freedoms?

"Often parents aren't home when their children are. Or they are too trusting about letting their children go places with other people."—Nicholas.

Think of your child's closest associate. Do you really know what they do when they are together?

"Secret dating can happen when parents are overly strict."—Paul.

Without compromising Bible laws and principles, how can you "let your reasonableness become known"?—Philippians 4:5.

"In my early teens, I had low self-esteem and I craved attention. I began e-mailing a boy in a neighboring congregation and fell in love. He made me feel special."—Linda.

Can you think of some healthier ways that Linda's needs could have been fulfilled at home?

Why not use Chapter 2 in Volume 2 as well as this section of the Appendix as a basis for discussion with your son or daughter? The best countermeasure to secrecy is heartfelt and forthright communication.—Proverbs 20:5.

How should I respond if my child talks about suicide?

In some parts of the world, suicide among the young is disturbingly common. For example, in the United States, suicide is the third leading cause of death among young people between the ages of 15 and 25, and during the past two decades, the suicide rate among those between the ages of 10 and 14 has doubled. Those most at risk include youths who suffer from a mental-health disorder, those who have a family history of suicide, and those who have attempted suicide in the past. Warning signs that a youth may be thinking of taking his or her life include the following:

SEE VOLUME 1, CHAPTERS 13 AND 14, AND VOLUME 2, CHAPTER 26

- Withdrawal from family and friends
- A change in eating and sleeping patterns
- A loss of interest in activities that were once pleasurable
- A marked change in personality
- Drug or alcohol abuse
- Giving away prized possessions
- Talking about death or being preoccupied with subjects related to it

One of the greatest mistakes a parent can make is to ignore such warning signs. Take all threats seriously. Do *not* hastily conclude that your child is simply going through a phase.

Also, don't be ashamed to get help for your son or daughter if he or she suffers from severe depression or another mental disorder. And if you suspect that your teen is thinking about ending it all, ask him or her about it. *The notion that a teen will be encouraged to commit suicide simply by talking about it is false.* Many youths are relieved when parents bring up the subject. So if your teen admits to having thoughts of suicide, find out if a plan has been devised, and if so, how detailed it is. The more detailed the plan, the more urgently you need to intervene.

Don't assume that the depression will lift on its own. And if it *does* seem to lift, don't think that the problem is solved. On the contrary, this could be the most dangerous point. Why? Because while in the throes of deep depression, an adolescent may be too immobilized to act on his or her suicidal feelings. However, when the dark feelings lift and energy returns, the youth may have the stamina to carry out the act.

It is indeed tragic that as a result of their despair, some youths consider ending it all. By being attentive to the signs and responding to them, parents and other caring adults may "speak consolingly to the depressed souls" and prove to be like a place of refuge for young ones.—1 Thessalonians 5:14.

Should I hide my grief from my children?

Grieving the loss of a mate is a painful experience. Yet it has come at a time when your adolescent child needs your

SEE VOLUME 1, CHAPTER 16

help. How can you help him to cope with his grief, while not ignoring your own?* Try the following:

● *Resist the urge to hide your feelings.* Your child has learned many of his most valuable lessons in life by watching you. Learning how to cope with grief will be no exception. Thus, do not feel that you must be strong for the child by hiding all your grief from him. This may only teach your son to do the same. In contrast, when you express your emotional pain, he learns that feelings are often better expressed than suppressed and that it is normal for him to feel saddened, frustrated, or even angry.

● *Encourage your adolescent to talk.* Without making him feel pressured, encourage your adolescent child to discuss what is in his heart. If he seems reluctant, why not discuss Chapter 16 of this volume? Also, talk about the many fond memories you have of your deceased mate. Acknowledge how difficult it will be for you to carry on. Hearing you express your feelings will help your adolescent learn how to do the same.

● *Recognize your limitations.* Understandably, you want to be an unfailing support for your adolescent child during this difficult time. But remember, you have been severely affected by the loss of your beloved mate. So your emotional, mental, and physical stamina may be somewhat diminished for a time. (Proverbs 24:10) Hence, you may need to call on the assistance of other adult family members and mature friends for support. Asking for help is a sign of maturity. Proverbs 11:2 says: "Wisdom is with the modest ones."

The best support you can have comes from Jehovah God himself, who promises his worshippers: "I, Jehovah your God, am grasping your right hand, the One saying to you, 'Do not be afraid. I myself will help you.'"—Isaiah 41:13.

---

* For simplicity, we refer to the child as a male. However, the principles discussed apply to both genders.

How can I help my daughter gain a balanced view of dieting?

If your daughter has fallen victim to an eating disorder, what can you do?* First, try to understand *why* she has resorted to this behavior.

It has been noted that many with eating disorders have a low self-image and are perfectionist in nature, setting unreasonably high expectations for themselves. Make sure that you do not contribute to those traits. Build up your daughter.—1 Thessalonians 5:11.

SEE VOLUME 1, CHAPTER 10, AND VOLUME 2, CHAPTER 7

Also take a close look at your own attitude toward food and weight. Have you unwittingly overemphasized these matters, either by word or by example? Remember, youths are extremely conscious of their appearance. Even teasing about "baby fat" or the normal growth spurt of adolescence can sow seeds of trouble in the mind of an impressionable youth.

Once you have prayerfully thought the matter through, have a heartfelt talk with your daughter. To do so, try the following:

- Plan carefully what to say and when to say it.

- Express clearly your concern and your desire to help.

- Do not be surprised if the first response is defensive.

- Be a patient listener.

Most important, become part of your daughter's efforts to get better. *Make recovery a family affair!*

---

* For simplicity, we refer to the child as a female. However, the principles discussed apply to both genders.

EMOTIONAL ISSUES

SPIRITUALITY

How can I continue to teach my children spiritual values as they enter adolescence?

The Bible says that Timothy was given spiritual training "from infancy," and as a parent, you have likely provided the same for your children. (2 Timothy 3:15) When your children become adolescents, however, your training methods may need to adapt to new circumstances. Your growing children are beginning to grasp complex, abstract issues that they could not fully comprehend when they were younger. Now more than ever, you'll need to appeal to their "power of reason."—Romans 12:1.

SEE VOLUME 1, CHAPTER 38, AND VOLUME 2, CHAPTERS 34-36

When writing to Timothy, Paul mentioned the things that Timothy had 'learned and was *persuaded* to believe.' (2 Timothy 3:14) Your adolescents may now need to be "persuaded to believe" the Bible truths that they have known since infancy. To reach their hearts, you need to do more than just tell them what to do or to believe. They need to learn for themselves. How can you help? Start by giving them plenty of opportunity to reason on and talk about such questions as the following:

● What convinces me that God exists?—Romans 1:20.

● How do I know that what I am being taught by my parents from the Bible is the truth?—Acts 17:11.

- What convinces me that Bible standards are for my own good?—Isaiah 48:17, 18.

- How do I know that Bible prophecies will be fulfilled? —Joshua 23:14.

- What convinces me that nothing in this world compares to "the excelling value of the knowledge of Christ Jesus"?—Philippians 3:8.

- What does Christ's ransom sacrifice mean to *me?* —2 Corinthians 5:14, 15; Galatians 2:20.

You might hesitate to have your adolescents ponder such questions, fearing that they won't be able to answer them. But that's like hesitating to look at the fuel gauge on your car's dashboard, fearing that it might be pointing to empty. If it is, it's best that you find out while you can do something about it! In the same way, now—while your adolescents are still at home—is the time to help them explore questions of faith and to become "persuaded to believe."*

Remember, there's nothing wrong with having your son or daughter ask, *"Why* do I believe?" Diane, 22, reflects on doing so as a teenager. "I didn't want to be insecure about my beliefs," she says. "Developing clear, firm answers made me realize that I *liked* being one of Jehovah's Witnesses! Whenever I was questioned about something that I wouldn't do, rather than replying, 'It's against my *religion,'* I would say, '*I* don't think it's right.' In other words, I made the Bible's view *my* view."

Suggestion: To tap into your adolescent's power of reason with regard to Bible standards, have him or her assume the role of the parent when a problem arises. For example, suppose your daughter has asked permission to

---

* Chapter 36 of Volume 2 can help adolescents use their reasoning powers to develop conviction that God exists.

attend a party that you (and likely she) knows would not be appropriate. Instead of simply responding with a no, you could say something like: 'What I'd like you to do is put yourself in my place. Think about the party you want to attend, do some research (perhaps Chapter 37 of this book and Chapter 32 of Volume 2), and then come back and talk to me tomorrow. I'll play your role and ask to go to this party, and in your role as the parent, you can tell me if it would be a good idea or not.'

Our teenager has lost interest in spiritual things. What can we do?

First, don't hastily conclude that your teen has *rejected your faith.* In many cases, there is an underlying issue. For example, perhaps your teen

- Is facing pressure from peers and is timid about standing out as different for adhering to Bible principles

- Sees other youths (even siblings) excelling at Christian living and feels that measuring up to them is impossible

- Is starving for friends but feels lonely or out of place among fellow believers

- Sees other "Christian" youths leading a double life

- Is striving to carve out a personal identity and as a result feels compelled to question the values you hold dear

- Sees classmates freely engaging in wrongdoing and seemingly not suffering any bad consequences

- Is trying to win the approval of a non-believing parent

SEE VOLUME 1, CHAPTER 39, AND VOLUME 2, CHAPTERS 37 AND 38

SPIRITUALITY

Significantly, issues such as these have little to do with the *tenets* of your faith. They have more to do with circumstances that make practicing faith a challenge—at least for now. So, what can you do to encourage your teen?

Make concessions—without compromising. Try to understand the cause of your adolescent's discouragement, and make adjustments so that your child will have a better environment in which to thrive spiritually. (Proverbs 16:20) For example, the "Peer-Pressure Planner" on pages 132 and 133 of Volume 2 can instill confidence in your child so that he or she is less timid about facing up to schoolmates. Or if your adolescent is lonely, you might need to take an active role in helping him or her find good associates.

Provide a mentor. Sometimes youths are helped when an adult outside the family provides encouragement. Do you know someone whose spiritual outlook could be an inspiration to your adolescent? Why not arrange for him or her to spend time with your son or daughter? Your purpose is not to abdicate your responsibility. But think of Timothy. He benefited greatly from the apostle Paul's example, and Paul benefited greatly by having Timothy as a companion. —Philippians 2:20, 22.

As long as your adolescent lives under your roof, you have the right to require compliance with a spiritual routine. In the end, however, your goal is to instill love for God in your teen's heart—not simply to elicit some mechanical action. To help your teen embrace true religion, set an example worthy of imitation. Be reasonable in what you expect. Provide a mentor and upbuilding associates. Perhaps one day your adolescent will be able to say, as did the psalmist, "Jehovah is *my* crag and *my* stronghold and the Provider of escape for *me*."—Psalm 18:2.

worksheet locator

More information online!
Log on to www.watchtower.org/ype

Would you welcome more information?

Write to Jehovah's Witnesses at the appropriate address below.

ALBANIA: PO Box 118, Tiranë. **ANGOLA:** Caixa Postal 6877, Luanda Sul. **ARGENTINA:** Casilla 83 (Suc 27B), C1427WAB Cdad. Aut. de Buenos Aires. **ARMENIA:** PO Box 75, 0010 Yerevan. **AUSTRALIA:** PO Box 280, Ingleburn, NSW 1890. **BAHAMAS:** PO Box N-1247, Nassau, NP. **BARBADOS, W.I.:** Crusher Site Road, Prospect, BB 24012 St. James. **BELGIUM:** rue d'Argile-Potaardestraat 60, B-1950 Kraainem. **BENIN:** 06 BP 1131, Akpakpa pk3, Cotonou. **BOLIVIA:** Casilla 6397, Santa Cruz. **BRAZIL:** CP 92, Tatuí-SP, 18270-970. **BRITAIN:** The Ridgeway, London NW7 1RN. **BULGARIA:** PO Box 424, 1618 Sofia. **BURKINA FASO:** 01 BP 1923, Ouagadougou 01. **BURUNDI:** BP 2150, Bujumbura. **CAMEROON:** BP 889, Douala. **CANADA:** PO Box 4100, Georgetown, ON L7G 4Y4. **CENTRAL AFRICAN REPUBLIC:** BP 662, Bangui. **CHILE:** Casilla 267, Puente Alto. **COLOMBIA:** Apartado 85058, Bogotá. **CONGO, DEMOCRATIC REPUBLIC OF:** BP 634, Limete, Kinshasa. **CÔTE D'IVOIRE:** 06 BP 393, Abidjan 06. **CROATIA:** PP 58, HR-10090 Zagreb-Susedgrad. **CURAÇAO, NETHERLANDS ANTILLES:** PO Box 4708, Willemstad. **DENMARK:** PO Box 340, DK-4300 Holbæk. **DOMINICAN REPUBLIC:** Apartado 1742, Santo Domingo. **ECUADOR:** Casilla 09-01-1334, Guayaquil. **ESTONIA:** PO Box 1075, 10302 Tallinn. **ETHIOPIA:** PO Box 5522, Addis Ababa. **FIJI:** PO Box 23, Suva. **FINLAND:** PO Box 68, FI-01301 Vantaa. **FRANCE:** BP 625, F-27406 Louviers Cedex. **GEORGIA:** PO Box 237, 0102 Tbilisi. **GERMANY:** 65617 Selters. **GHANA:** PO Box GP 760, Accra. **GREECE:** Kifisias 77, GR 151 24 Marousi. **GUAM:** 143 Jehovah St, Barrigada, GU 96913. **GUINEA:** BP 2714, Conakry 1. **GUYANA:** 352-360 Tyrell St, Republic Park Phase 2 EBD. **HAITI:** PO Box 185, Port-au-Prince. **HONG KONG:** 4 Kent Road, Kowloon Tong, Kowloon. **HUNGARY:** Budapest, Pf 20, H-1631. **INDIA:** PO Box 6441, Yelahanka, Bangalore-KAR 560 064. **INDONESIA:** PO Box 2105, Jakarta 10001. **ISRAEL:** PO Box 29345, 61293 Tel Aviv. **ITALY:** Via della Bufalotta 1281, I-00138 Rome RM. **JAMAICA:** PO Box 103, Old Harbour, St. Catherine. **JAPAN:** 4-7-1 Nakashinden, Ebina City, Kanagawa-Pref, 243-0496. **KAZAKHSTAN:** PO Box 198, Almaty, 050000. **KENYA:** PO Box 21290, Nairobi 00505. **KOREA, REPUBLIC OF:** PO Box 33, Pyungtaek PO, Kyunggi-do, 450-600. **KYRGYZSTAN:** PO Box 80, 720080 Bishkek. **LATVIA:** A.k. 15, Rīga, LV-1001. **LIBERIA:** PO Box 10-0380, 1000 Monrovia 10. **LITHUANIA:** Pd 2632, LT-48022 Kaunas. **MACEDONIA:** Pf 800, 1000 Skopje. **MADAGASCAR:** BP 116, 105 Ivato. **MALAWI:** PO Box 30749, Lilongwe 3. **MALAYSIA:** Peti Surat No. 580, 75760 Melaka. **MEXICO:** Apartado Postal 895, 06002 Mexico, DF. **MOLDOVA, REPUBLIC OF:** PO Box 472, MD-2005 Chişinău. **MOZAMBIQUE:** PO Box 2600, 1100 Maputo. **MYANMAR:** PO Box 62, Yangon. **NEPAL:** PO Box 24438, GPO, Kathmandu. **NETHERLANDS:** Noordbargerstraat 77, NL-7812 AA Emmen. **NEW CALEDONIA:** BP 1741, 98874 Pont des Français. **NEW ZEALAND:** PO Box 75142, Manurewa, Manukau 2243. **NIGERIA:** PMB 1090, Benin City 300001, Edo State. **NORWAY:** Gaupeveien 24, NO-1914 Ytre Enebakk. **PAPUA NEW GUINEA:** PO Box 636, Boroko, NCD 111. **PARAGUAY:** Casilla 482, 1209 Asunción. **PERU:** Apartado 18-1055, Lima 18. **PHILIPPINES:** PO Box 2044, 1060 Manila. **POLAND:** ul. Warszawska 14, PL-05830 Nadarzyn. **PORTUGAL:** Apartado 91, P-2766-955 Estoril. **PUERTO RICO:** PO Box 3980, Guaynabo, PR 00970. **ROMANIA:** PO Box 132, OP 39, Bucureşti. **RUSSIA:** PO Box 182, 190000 St. Petersburg. **RWANDA:** BP 529, Kigali. **SAMOA:** PO Box 673, Apia. **SENEGAL:** BP 29896, 14523 Dakar. **SERBIA:** PO Box 173, SRB 11080 Beograd/Zemun. **SIERRA LEONE:** PO Box 136, Freetown. **SLOVAKIA:** PO Box 2, 830 04 Bratislava 34. **SLOVENIA:** pp 22, SI-1241 Kamnik. **SOLOMON ISLANDS:** PO Box 166, Honiara. **SOUTH AFRICA:** Private Bag X2067, Krugersdorp, 1740. **SPAIN:** Apartado 132, 28850 Torrejón de Ardoz (Madrid). **SRI LANKA:** 711 Station Road, Wattala 11300. **SUDAN:** PO Box 957, 11111, Khartoum. **SURINAME:** PO Box 2914, Paramaribo. **SWEDEN:** PO Box 5, SE-732 21 Arboga. **TAHITI, FRENCH POLYNESIA:** BP 7715, 98719 Taravao. **TAIWAN:** 3-12, Shetze Village, Hsinwu 32746. **TANZANIA:** PO Box 7992, Dar es Salaam. **THAILAND:** PO Box 7 Klongchan, Bangkok 10 240. **TRINIDAD AND TOBAGO:** Lower Rapsey Street & Laxmi Lane, Curepe. **TURKEY:** PO Box 23, Feriköy, 34378 İstanbul. **UGANDA:** PO Box 4019, Kampala. **UKRAINE:** PO Box 955, 79491 Lviv - Briukhovychi. **UNITED STATES OF AMERICA:** 25 Columbia Heights, Brooklyn, NY 11201-2483. **URUGUAY:** Casilla 17030, César Mayo Gutiérrez 2645 y Cno. Varzi, 12500 Montevideo. **VENEZUELA:** Apartado 20.364, Caracas, DC 1020A. **ZAMBIA:** PO Box 33459, 10101 Lusaka. **ZIMBABWE:** Private Bag WG-5001, Westgate.   www.watchtower.org